TWELVE 1 TO SUCCESS

BOXING STRATEGIES FOR
PERSONAL ACHIEVEMENT AND BUSINESS

Written by:

Michael L. Moorer

3 Time Heavyweight Boxing Champion of the World

Introduction by:

George Foreman

Heavyweight Boxing Champion of the World

Co-Author:

Walter F. Philbrick

Warning & Disclaimer

This book was written and published to help you succeed personally and financially. I had personal success in boxing and won the Heavy weight championship of the world on three different occasions. This book is about what it takes to succeed in life and boxing. In this book I will parallel boxing, life and operating a business. I will tell the reader several personal stories and some of my experiences on what it takes to be successful and improve the quality of your life.

The chapters or twelve rounds to success are the important principles I used to achieve my personal goals. Everyone has different goals and alternative methods for achievement. This disclaimer is just to let the readers know that everyone's level of success will be measured differently. Some leaders in the business world will not feel personally satisfied unless they are the CEO of a fortune 500 corporation. While another person's dream is to be the manager of a local McDonald's restaurant or to own their own home. Everyone's success is measured differently.

Some people will achieve success and be content with being able to afford a house and a car that is less than five years old. Everyone will seek and attain different levels of their own success. Remember, your personal success can also be measured financially, personally, socially, physically, spiritually and in many other ways. To each his own dream.

This book has been written integrating my boxing career, personal stories and my experiences. The reader must realize that each event will be different in your life. Therefore the author(s) assumes no liability or responsibility for the use or content of this book.

I wish I was there to guide you through each chapter or round but obviously I can't be there. Only you as an individual can set your levels of success and achieve your personal goals. Therefore, you are on your own to achieve and build your own personnel dreams and levels of success.

Introduction
By George Foreman

Michael L. Moorer and I have both won the Heavyweight Boxing Championship of the World on more than one occasion. Few men can claim that accomplishment. Michael Moorer is the only boxer in history to win the heavyweight title being a southpaw. Southpaw means you fight left handed with your right hand forward and your left hand is your power hand. When I fought Michael the southpaw stance made it difficult for me to hit him.

He has a professional record of 50 wins, 4 losses and one draw. Michael Moorer's first loss was when we fought for the heavyweight title in 1994 in Las Vegas, Nevada. Looking back on that night it was one of the hardest and most difficult fights of my boxing career. Remember, I fought all the boxing greats. Just to name a few were Muhammad Ali and "Smokin" Joe Frazier. Those were some of the best boxers in the business.

It has been almost 20 years since Double "M" or Michael Moorer and I fought for the Heavyweight Boxing Championship of the World. This was a great opportunity for me to fight again for the title. I had several months to prepare for the fight. I wanted the title back. If I could only do it one more time. I wanted to show the world that George Foreman could still win the heavyweight crown. I was 45 years old that cool night in Las Vegas.

What people do not remember about my opponent that night was that Michael Moorer had one of the longest strings of consecutive knockouts in boxing history. He had risen through the light heavyweight ranks and knocked out all of his 22 opponents in a row over a span of four years. That by itself is boxing history. At this time he was undefeated and in the prime of his life.

I was again fighting for the Heavyweight Championship of the World and here I was a grandfather. Not your typical professional boxer.

The fight started off well for me but in the later rounds I began to tire. Michael was beginning to pound me.

He was ahead on the scorecards and I was losing. Michael Moorer was a worthy opponent. He had just beaten Evander Holyfield for the title.

We were both warriors that night but only one of us could be victorious. My success that night was his failure. There are no second places in boxing. This would absolutely be my last fight, win or lose. We both wanted to win. I wanted the title and he wanted to keep it. Michael had never lost a fight prior to this night. He had 36 consecutive wins with no losses. I had my work cut out for me.

I hate to say it but I was the old dog. I was old, but still had a little left. At the beginning of the 10th round my trainer, Angelo Dundee grabbed me and said, "You're losing; you need to knock this guy out." I needed a miracle.

It was the 10th round and I was way behind on all the score cards. I needed a knockout or I was going to lose. I reached down deep inside myself and gathered all of the energy and power I had left and I waited. I waited for that small window of opportunity when he dropped his right hand. I was tired and he was winning. That's when I saw it. With every ounce of strength remaining in my body I hit Michael Moorer, the reigning heavyweight champion of the world. I hit him with two (2) combinations and a straight right hand and down he went. Michael was not getting up.

Later I learned that the right hand knockout punch cut Michael's lip and he needed 34 stitches to close the cut. I had just won the heavyweight championship title again at 45 years old! I was truly a blessed man. It was one of the most exciting days of my life.

Why do I tell you this story, because Michael and I have sacrificed years of our lives to become world champions? You don't wear the heavyweight crown or any crown for that matter unless you have sacrificed part of your life.

Do you remember the "Rumble in the jungle?" It was October 30, 1974. I got knocked out by Muhammad Ali in Zaire, Africa. I know how embarrassing it is to get up off the canvas after getting knocked out. The heavyweight title fight is being watched by millions of people around the world.

To get to that night takes more than skill, determination or sacrifice. It takes the spirit of a warrior. Michael Moorer and I have a lot in common. We both have gotten up off the canvas after being knocked out. We may have been beaten but not defeated.

Now, there is the story, here is the point. After the fight and during my interview with Larry Merchant I told him, "If you wish upon a star your dreams can come true. Don't give up on your dream." We both dreamed of doing it and we did it. We were both Heavyweight Boxing Champions of the World. Michael Moorer just prior to our fight had beaten the invincible Evander Holyfield who held the title.

We have both reached the pinnacle of success in our profession. We both at one time in our lives, held the World Heavyweight Boxing title. We were successful in our journey to the top. How many people can say that?

But here is why I offered to write the introduction to Michael Moorer's book on 12 Rounds to Success. What is important in life is what you do after a set back or you have lost the title. Learn from your mistakes. The Dalai Lama says, "When you lose, don't lose the lesson." Michael Moorer and I have been to the top and both of us have gotten up after being knocked out. Still we are successful in life.

Don't measure your life or your personal success on how much money you have. My life revolves around my family, religion and my businesses. You can have as much as you want, if you are only willing to work for it.

As you get older you will discover that your life is really measured in moments. The birth of your first child, getting that part in your first movie or the company promotion that will put you over the top. You have to work so hard for those moments. Cherish them.

Success in this life is attainable. You can be a success if you are the CEO of a large company, being a good father or husband or a great leader. Find your own personal level of success. Take the time to read this book and it will improve the quality of your life.

I made more money after boxing than I did as a professional boxer. That night in Las Vegas changed my life. If I had not beaten my friend Michael Moorer you would be eating and grilling off the Michael Moorer lean cooking grill and not the George Foreman grill. Michael is now in the second phase of his life, after the ring. I wish him luck with his book and any other ventures he pursues.

One thing you should not forget is that every day is important. Make every day in your life count. Find your eternal peace and make something of your life. One moment in time, one second or one punch can change your life forever. Have you prepared yourself? God bless you.

George Foreman

Preface
By Michael Moorer

This book chronicles my life as a boxer and my success track getting there. I was a professional boxer for over 20 years and during that time experienced success and failure in and out of the ring.

I retired from boxing in 2009 and now own an investigative agency. I am also a paid guest speaker at motivational and business seminars, executive conferences and charity functions. At the seminars, I talk about success and how to get there. Making money as a boxer or as a business professional are not that far apart. Professional boxing and the road to success parallel each other. You do not become successful unless you have the necessary qualities to make it happen.

This book will take you through the steps to being a winner and becoming successful in your life. Just because you are a winner today that doesn't guarantee you success tomorrow. Look at the many famous movie actors who commit suicide and boxers who were at the top and are now at the bottom financially.

It doesn't matter who you are or where you are in life, you can still be successful. You can be an entrepreneur, a successful business man or business woman. You can own your own corporation or just work for someone. It doesn't matter what you do as long as you rise to your level of success. Everyone can find success in their own way.

That day may come when you look in the mirror and ask yourself, "Am I really satisfied with whom I am and where I am in my life?" Are you happy? Have you found love? Do I have enough money? Am I a good worker, father husband? The list goes on forever. But what is important here is this is the first step to your success because you are now challenging yourself. You realize that you must change to achieve what you truly deserve and want in this life.

Financial success, being a leader or buying a new house are goals. To achieve these goals you must acquire and possess certain qualities. Achieving success just doesn't happen. There is very little luck in becoming successful. It takes hard work and certain qualities to get to the top of your profession.

Being successful is a combination of twelve qualities that separates the winners from losers. If you learn and practice these 12 steps in this book they can make you a better business person and a hopefully a champion in life. The 12 steps are outlined in this book are called rounds. In this book I call the sections rounds and not chapters. Why, because there are always twelve (12) rounds in a championship fight, thus 12 rounds to your success.

In the book, I detail some of my personal experiences as a boxer and being Heavyweight Champion of the World. You will see life through my eyes as a boxer. My style was different and I was gifted. I had success early in my career by boxing "south paw." I also thank God for being born with good genes and being able to throw a good punch. It has been said by sports commentators that my punch could make mountains crumble. I'm just a humble man who had a small piece of boxing history.

The book focuses on the parallels of being a professional boxer and being in business. It is the exact same thing as being an executive in a large corporation or going 10 rounds in the ring. The management and leadership traits are the same.

The book is a step-by-step model for success. People will buy and read the book for different reasons. You might want to increase your income, improve your status at work or just find a different direction in your life. This book can help you find success in all of these areas. Remember, success is more than just financial. It can also be family, personal relationships, religious, and your physical and mental well-being.

Here's a thought. Make a daily or weekly plan to read the book. After reading the book, you will discover the secret to being successful. You will learn what separates winners from losers. I have outlined the steps for you to follow. It's really simple and everyone who reads the book can get positive results that could change your life.

In the book, I have quoted men and woman who personally forged nations, built empires, and have inspired millions of people with their teaching. I even made up a few quotes of my own. You can do that if you write your own book. Some of the quotes are on life, some on business but all of them have a purpose to hopefully inspire you. Most of the quotes are from great leaders and men who changed history.

I promise you that if you apply some of the principles from this book to your daily life, I guarantee you positive results. You can become successful and have a better life for yourself and your family.

Michael L. Moorer

Table of Contents

ROUND 1
Get Motivated

"Before you can understand, motivate, and lead others, you must first understand, motivate and lead yourself."

—*Paul Meyer*

This book is a guide to becoming successful. Twelve Rounds to success is a step-by-step process for you to improve your life. It is a 12-point plan that helped me move through the boxing ranks of the light heavyweight division to finally fighting for the Heavy Weight Championship of the World. If you follow the steps, it will and can improve your life.

You might not become the heavyweight champion of the world but you can become successful. You will find that very small changes in your life over several years produce incredible results. You might find success by being the owner of your own business, an executive of a fortune 500 company, losing 50 pounds, or managing your favorite restaurant. You can have anything in this life, if you are willing to work for it.

If you are motivated you can be somebody and make a difference in your world. The purpose of life is to live it. If you change your life it changes your dynamics and the lives of others around you. Don't let other people determine your destiny. Take control of your destiny. It's all about you and where you want to be one day.

Motivation is just a word if you don't get your motors going. Decide what you want out of your life and go for it. It's what you want to do, not what other people want you to do! Now that you are motivated, I am going to ask you a question, "How bad do you want it and are you willing to very work hard to get it?"

It doesn't matter where you are today but where you end up 3-5 years from now.

> *Muhammad Ali once told a group of troubled teenagers, "If they can make penicillin out of moldy bread, they can sure make something out of you."*

The Weather

It is up to you, your decision, how you feel every day. You can decide to be sad, happy, motivated, jealous or resentful. I want you to be your personal weatherman but the difference is, you can decide the weather around you. Can you imagine being able to decide how the day is going to begin and end. Today I am going to be happy and get a lot of work done. That is exactly what I want you to do. You can choose sunshine, rain, storms, snow or cold. This can be your attitude and your motivation for the day. Why not chose the best weather and see what happens.

Now, what will make your day better? You can be distraught or proactive. You can choose to be happy with sunshine or be miserable with a cold weather day. It's all your decision. You now have a choice on how your day is going to begin.

If you get the same bad weather everyday it is because you didn't change or the environment around you remained the same. You will find that the way you feel impacts and influences the people around you.

Try it one day. Walk into work and say, "Wow, what a beautiful day. It's great to be alive, I love coming to work!" Immediately your employees and friends will feed off your optimism and you will see an immediate change in your staff. Keep doing it and after a while that change can be measureable in production and profits.

> *"Being cheerful keeps you healthy."*

> —*King Solomon*

I Have a Dream

It all begins with a dream. Who you are and where you want to be in 10 years. You have to start somewhere. You have to visualize it first before you can do it. Martin Luther King <u>didn't say</u>, "I have a plan." Of course not he said, "I have a dream." He saw the future of America. Unfortunately his life was cut short by an assassin.

Are you cutting your life short by drinking, using drugs and not being healthy? Do you have a gift or potential you are not using? These are immediate changes you can make in yourself. What is your dream? Don't be afraid to dare to be great. Just maybe, it can become reality.

"People can succeed at almost anything for which they have unlimited enthusiasm."

—Charles Schwab

How Do I get to be Successful?

There are two parts to the equation of being successful. The first part of being successful is just showing up. What does that mean? It may take years for you to get there but now you are there. You are at the point of making it big. Will Rogers said, "Even if you're on the right track, you'll get run over if you just sit there."

The other half knows what to do when they get there. This is done by getting the skills to move forward. Sometimes you already possess these skills and don't even know it. Decide what you want to do and go out and do it.

Success does not and will not come easy. If you are <u>not</u> satisfied with your financial or economical status, then do something about it. A friend of mine, "Vinnie" wants to meet girls and hopefully have a girlfriend. The problem is he goes to work and goes home every night. What does he think is going to happen? A gorgeous girl is just going to show up at his front door and say, "I heard you were looking for a girlfriend, well here I am." Of course not, that will never happen. Vinnie does absolutely nothing to change his life or present situation. Success and happiness is not going to come to you. You have to go out and get it.

Author unknown: "Don't be afraid to go out on a limb... that is where the fruit is."

Success and You

Some people are just gifted with size and strength. They are born with the physical qualities and genetics to become a professional athlete. Most of these athletes don't end up playing the violin at Carnegie Hall in New York or singing in a rock band. They end up playing professional football or other professional sports. Not everyone wants to play professional sports and not all of us are given that physical talent.

Are you gifted? Do you have the physical or mental qualities to excel? The teaching point here is, they maximized on what they are good at and also what they enjoy doing.

The question is, "What do you enjoy doing?" The second question is "What are you good at?" You have to make a decision like the professional athlete, carpenter, waiter or movie actor. Decide what you enjoy doing. Remember you can always build some skills that can make you successful.

What do you like doing and do you have any skills? It really is that simple but of course it is going to be risky. You are not guaranteed that you will be successful. But, whatever you do, be committed. Like the professional poker player in Las Vegas, say to yourself, "I'm all in."

I had the passion to box. I was good at boxing and improved my skills everyday in the gym. It doesn't matter what you choose to do, just love doing it! Remember, you can't change your physical size but you can always improve your skills.

Kentucky Fried Chicken (KFC) owner Colonel Sanders loved to cook and had an incredible recipe for fried chicken. He had no money but had a potentially great product. As history tells the story, he went to over one-hundred restaurants before one owner took a chance and cooked his fried chicken with the secret recipe. Today KFC is one of the largest franchise restaurants in the world. Find something you love to do and you will never work another day in your life.

"People who are <u>unable</u> to motivate themselves must be content with mediocrity, no matter how impressive their other talents are."

—*Andrew Carnegie*

Passion for What You Do

A key trait shared by successful people is their passion for what they are doing. Since I was 10 years old, I knew in my heart what I wanted to be. I wanted to be a professional boxer. That was my goal and what I dreamed of every day of my life. Actors love to act and musicians love the audience. I wanted to be a fighter.

My grandfather was a trainer and a professional boxer. He had a few fights, but his career didn't go anywhere so he decided to help other boxers become better fighters. He would make me work in the yard all day and after I finished, only then would he take me to the boxing gym with him. That is where my passion for boxing began. The love of anything starts out slow but it grows rapidly. I loved boxing and I knew what my destiny was.

I could never see myself going to a job I absolutely hated. If you are in that position now I am going to show you how to make the change and have success in your life.

Decide to Change

One of the first things you have to do is make your mind up to change. Say to yourself, "I'm done with this job! I am going to change." You must want to change and have the internal fire to make that decision that will hopefully give you a better life. No one says it's going to be easy but make the decision and don't look back.

Look forward to going to the gym, attending that business meeting or making that sales call. It's all about enthusiasm in everything you do. Sure, you are saying, "Wait a minute Michael Moorer you were champion of the world." That is true but I loved every minute of my climb to the top. I loved the cold icy 20 degree runs at 5:00 a.m. in the morning in Pittsburgh. I enjoyed the physical conditioning all day and then going to the gym that night to prepare for a fight. Well, okay, I really didn't like the cold morning runs but the rest I did enjoy.

When I decided to change and dedicate my life to a boxing career that change didn't occur overnight. It is a process. The decision you make and I made does change your life. As a young man, I had to sacrifice and I missed the growing up period of being a teenager. There were no dances, parties, vacations, close friends and very few girlfriends. My life was boxing and nothing more.

It's all relative to where you want to finish in life. Remember, life is a onetime event. You only get one chance. Make the best of it. Use your God given talents and find your passion. If you never try, how do you know what could have happened? You could have been successful. You might become a millionaire.

Who knows? Get out there and try. If you continue to do absolutely nothing, there will be no change. Get the power of passion. Let's all finish on top.

"We may affirm absolutely, that nothing great in the world has ever been accomplished without passion."

—Hegel

Business is ShowTime

Boxing fans or your customers, it's all the same. It's all about business and taking care of the customer. Have you been to a fight where the boxers jab a little, do some dancing and really don't mix it up? What do the fans do? They boo the fighters. Boxing or a comedy or star studded show is exactly the same. If I don't put on a good show in the ring, people will not come back to see me. It's show time whether you're in business or a boxer.

I was not good at putting on a show before a fight. Once in the ring I took care of business. You don't know me but I'm really a quiet person. I'm not much on flash, bling or bragging. I kept it to myself and let my gloves do the talking in the ring. My show began after the bell rang for the first round.

Iron Mike Tyson was a great example of a good show. He would come into the ring wearing just a towel. He didn't have any fancy warm-up suits or a huge bunch of bodyguards. Just Iron Mike, his fight team and a towel. Then what would he do? He would crush his opponent with a flurry of punches and then his famous uppercut. It was simple but effective and very entertaining. When it is your time to shine, light up the world.

Rich or Happy

You will not always find happiness when you have money. I admit that it does help to have a few dollars in the bank but money alone will not make you happy. What makes you content, satisfied and happy are five things:

- Personal satisfaction of who you are
- Being healthy
- Your family and friends (Personal relationships)
- Love what you are doing
- The feeling that your life matters (personally and religiously)
- Being able to provide for your family

You will only find success if you have balance in your life. I can truthfully say that from experience. My personal and family life were difficult at times during my boxing career. Traveling and training took up most of my days. Finding time for my family was always a challenge.

For example, if you are successful in your chosen career but after work you go home to a dysfunctional family, that doesn't work? You need balance in your life.

If one part of your life is out of sync, it will affect the other areas of your life. That is why your foundation begins with your home and your health. Your foundation must support what you are doing. Without a good foundation, even the tallest buildings collapse.

Health Matters

If you are not healthy, you will not enjoy your life. I will repeat that, "If you are not physically healthy you cannot enjoy the true enjoyment of life."

From professional boxing, I have had a total of 16 surgeries on my hands, arms and shoulders. Prior to my last professional fight in Dubai, my right hand hurt so badly, I could hardly hold a cup of coffee. I fought anyway and won.

It's been almost 3 years now and my hand has healed. My knees are better and I'm in good health. I feel like boxing again.

The only problem is if I did decide to fight again my body does not heal like it did when I was in my twenties. After the Foreman fight the hospital stitched the inside of my lip up but few people know that my internal organs also bled. George's body shots didn't affect me during the fight but the following day I had blood in my urine for over six days. In my forties, my body just would not recover fast enough to have any type of career. Mentally I still have the warrior spirit but physically it is just not there anymore.

To reach your full potential you must take care of yourself physically and mentally. Remember, the mind controls the body. We all know what it takes to get in shape and take care of our bodies, but again it's that matter of discipline. Health does matters. We will discuss getting healthy later in the book.

Enjoy what you do

If you truly love what you do then make it your profession. The next step is to master what you do. What that means is take your profession to the next step. Learn everything you can about what you do. Start your own company and excel in the field that you have chosen.

Studies on careers and employment have shown that most people will change their profession 3-4 times during their lifetime. Sounds like some of my friends and the number of times they have been married and divorced. Why do we change careers or get divorced? It is because we are not happy with what we are presently doing. Sometimes it's not the money. It is enjoying what you do for a living. How would you feel if you looked forward to going to work every day? It would be like me dreading my next fight. Oh, I don't want to fight Mike Tyson. Do you think that would affect how I train for the fight? It's all relative. It is up to you to make that change from a job you hate, to doing something you love.

This book is not only about financial success but personal success. If you find personal success, many times financial gains are not far behind. Maybe you want to lose weight or find your soul mate. The book outlines principals on achieving those goals. Losing weight or changing jobs will affect your life.

That is what this book is all about. Is it easy to change jobs? "No." Is it easy to lose weight? "No." It's going to be hard, very hard in the beginning. You will adjust and look back one day and say, "Yes, I did it." After a short time you will see a difference in your life. Other people will also take notice that you have taken control of your life and decided to change.

You can make a profession out of just about anything. If you want inner peace then start a career that helps people. I loved boxing because I was a warrior. To me it was the physical combat between two individuals that kept me in the sport. Here is a very important point. If you choose a profession that you love, you will never run out of passion.

Even though I have not fought in a few years, the passion to get back in the ring keeps bringing me back to boxing. Maybe I am too old (George wasn't too old when he clobbered me) to fight so now I train new fighters. It's kind of like, I have gone from student to now master, where I teach the art of boxing. I find it challenging and rewarding to take a fighter with potential and teach him the skills of boxing.

Hope

By buying this book and reading the chapters it shows me that you want to change your life. It all begins with hope. Did you ever buy a lottery ticket? Maybe you spent $5 on this week's Mega Ball Lottery or your state lottery. If you win it will pay over 138 million dollars. The funny thing is that when you bought that lottery ticket deep down inside you had this feeling," Maybe this is it. This is the one, the winning ticket to my fortune." Of course you didn't win but you had hope. But, for that brief second or two there was hope.

That's where it begins with motivating yourself for success. It is that exact same feeling when you bought that lottery ticket. If you didn't buy a ticket you will never have had that chance to win. At least now you have a chance of winning. If you don't try, you will never change your life.

Hope Turns to Passion

You must imagine that you can do it. Think outside the box. Move from where you are today to where you truly want to be. Have a goal for everyday. Each day I want you to perform an action that takes you a little bit closer to your goal. Get something accomplished. The size of the goal doesn't matter. It could be as simple as getting a haircut and changing the way you look. That is one-step in your transition for change.

It doesn't do any good to write down the goal of the day and not complete it. Whatever it takes, get that goal completed. An analogy of setting goals would be if you were a ship captain, rather than set a course each day you just sailed around in circles. At the end of the day you didn't make any progress in crossing the ocean. Then you would return to your port each night. You should have planned goals for each day otherwise you are just sailing around in circles.

This action is short term obviously but it is positive movement toward your success. It might be as small as reading the periodicals or Success Magazine to re-energize you. The key is that each day you start building and working toward your personal goal. If you do this your enthusiasm and excitement will build. Why, because now you have hope for a change in your life.

One day when you're working toward your dream or vision, hope will turn into passion. Hope is a dream. Passion is a driving force that sustains love, makes men champions and is the fuel for the fire. When dreams turn into reality, your success level will accelerate. Why, because now you love what you are doing.

Get Started Today

Walt Disney said it best, "If you can dream it, you can do it." The key is just getting started. Determine where you want to be five (5) years from now and get started today. When is the best time in your life to begin your new profession? Why not today?

As we grow time seems to race at incredible intervals. Five years ago seems like yesterday. You're in your twenties today and tomorrow you wake up and your forty-five years old. That is how fast time goes by. This new program you are starting will keep you busy. That is why it is so important to get started as soon as possible. In no time, months will go by and you will be one step closer to your dreams.

What is important is that each day you move closer towards your goals, one day at a time, never missing a day. Don't procrastinate. Get that daily planner and write down exactly what you are going to do today and next week. Get something done each and every day, no matter how small. Be very specific on the daily task. Once it is completed, mark it off. These are small steps toward changing your future.

Did you know that 96% of all adults from 25 to 44 years of age have looked into starting their own business? But in the end less than half of that total took the chance and started their own company. It is also a fact that 74% of the millionaires in America own their own business. Isn't it about time you take control of your life rather than let life control you. Don't let things happen, make it happen. Get motivated and start today.

Excuse me for using so many quotes but I really enjoy the oriental philosophy. Confucius said, "And remember, no matter where you go, there you are." This is very simple in translation and understanding.

It doesn't matter how old you are. You can be ten years old or sixty-five years old. Ask yourself, what do I want to do with my life? What standard of quality do I want for my family and myself? Am I content with where I am financially, socially and economically? What am I doing and where am I going? These are decisions you have to make. My personal philosophy has always been, "Don't ask me what I have done, but ask me what I'm going to do tomorrow."

The key is to just to get started. It was the same philosophy for me in writing this book. You can think about it all the time but the only meaningful time is when you sit down and start doing it. So one day I started putting my story into words rather than thoughts. It starts with one page at a time. The point is to do something every day. You may have to motivate yourself just to start but once you gain momentum, the rest is easy.

If you ever decide you want to write a book here is how you do it. I want you to write just one page every day. That's it. Every day sit down and write just one single page. At the end of the year you will have written 365 pages. That is a pretty good start to getting your novel or book completed.

Motivation Is Not Enough

You can be inspired, motivated and have tons of passion but nothing gets done unless you take action. Taking action is the first step towards success. It is the mental commitment to get started that separates the winners from the losers.

As a boxer, the training regiment is extremely tough. Every day you are on a strict diet, nutritional plan, the miles of roadwork of running every morning at 4:00 a.m., sit ups, hitting the bag, sparring and more. But, once I get started I gain enthusiasm and momentum. The key is to get through that first week of training camp and that's when I know I'm on my way.

This is how you get started. Motivation is great but until you make that first PAS or progressive action step, you have done nothing. Make that commitment, set a date and just begin. It is the action of moving forward, rather than standing still that makes us all winners. Commitment is the key to becoming successful.

Fear as a Motivator

When I made my living as a professional boxer, I was highly motivated not to get my head knocked off my shoulders. However, looking back at all the fights and some of the beatings I took; I can say, "I never gave up."

Vince Lombardi the famous coach of the Green Bay Packers and one of the all time greats said, "We didn't lose the game, we just ran out of time." Coach Lombardi does not want to acknowledge defeat. The football coach always professed a motivating attitude.

I believe what motivated me more than the money was the fear of failure…..the fear of just getting beat. I had never been beaten until I fought George Foreman and I should have won that fight. I was not motivated by the money or fame. What kept me going was I just hated to lose at something I really loved.

Today I look back and think what might have been if I had beaten big George that night in Las Vegas. This would be my sixth book rather than my first book. I should have won the fight, but that is history. It is good to reflect on your experiences as a learning tool. Learn from your defeats but do not dwell on them. If you live in the past you will never see the future. Learn from it, forget it and move forward.

Ask yourself, "What motivates me?" Is it for the money, sex, fame, or your inner strength and desire to excel? Inspiration can come from someone else but determination and motivation must come from within you.

Goal Specific

Ask yourself this, "What would I do in my life if I knew I could not fail?" Now this thought has some limitations. For example, if you are 5'2" in height and you want to be on the Orlando Magic professional basketball team that probably is not going to happen. Although there was one professional basketball player named Buggsy Bogues who was 5'3" and played professional basketball for several years. I want you to be realistic and chose a goal or career that you can make happen.

So your goal may be, "I want to be a millionaire." Did you know that 7% of households in the United States are millionaires? Also that 80% of the rich in America earned the money themselves and only 20% inherited it. You can do it if you just follow the guidelines in this book.

What if you wanted to run your own company and make more money? Let's say right now your occupation is painting houses for a living and you want more out of life.

What are your options?

1) Work 16 hours a day and paint twice as many houses.
2) Work weekends to make that extra income you want.
3) Learn the house painting business and start your own company.

You might be the only employee in your business for years but if you do a professional job on every house you paint, that satisfied customer is your best sales representative. You will get referrals and his business again. Soon you will have to hire someone to help you and the following year hopefully you are painting six houses a week with three painting teams on the road. The point is to have a directional goal. Know what you want and start moving in that direction.

In the next quote by Virgil, he refers to constantly thinking about what you want to be. All day and all night you think about one thing. It has been proven that you soon become what you think about most.

"They can because they think they can."

—Virgil- Poet and author in the middle ages

Key Points of Round 1: Get Motivated

- Decide on what you want to do
- Write it down and be specific and clear
- What is your motivation for the change
- Get excited about it and get started today
- If you don't try you are automatically a failure
- Begin to think about how you are going to change
- Start to get healthy

Progressive Action Steps (PAS)   Completed

1. I have decided on what I want to do.   ☐

2. I am now creating a plan to get there.   ☐

3. I have decided on a plan of action.   ☐

4. I can and I will achieve my goals.   ☐

<u>ROUND 2</u>
Have a Plan and Set Goals

"If you don't know where you are going, how are you going to get there?" New York Yankees Baseball Player and Coach."

—*Yogi Berra*

I congratulate you on finishing the first round or chapter one. Now that you are motivated it's time to set goals and develop a plan. Round one has you moving in the right direction. You are motivated and have written down some short term and long-term goals. You are now ready to move forward and develop a plan to reach those objectives.

Develop a Plan

It is a proven fact that people will spend more time planning their summer vacation than their lives. Successful people plan while others just plan to get through tomorrow. If you develop a plan and follow it, you can and will become successful. Once you have developed a plan, the second most important thing is to implement that plan.

When I was a young boy I use to watch the boxing greats on TV. Just some of them were Joe Frazier, Ken Norton and of course the king Muhammad Ali. I wasn't born when Muhammad Ali won the Heavyweight Boxing Championship of the World but I always respected him as a fighter. I have used several of his quotes in this book. He is quite the philosopher.

But my real hero was Marvin Hagler. He was a southpaw like me and we both boxed bald. Watching Marvelous Marvin Hagler gave me direction on what I wanted to do with my life. I wanted to be like my hero, Marvin Hagler and win the middleweight boxing championship of the world. I had a goal but no plan.

You can have all of the motivation and enthusiasm in the world, but if you do not have a plan or a road map to get there, you will not succeed. Would you go on vacation and just get in your car and say to your spouse, where do you want to go and just drive around? That is what many people are doing with their lives. They have no goals and do not have a road map to success. They just drive around and see where life takes them. That is not what successful people do. Find out where you want to go and move in that direction.

Written Goals

During my first years as a professional boxer, I actually lived in the basement of my trainer. His name was Emanuel Stewart. His house in Detroit was modest but adequate. I was just thankful to have a place to stay and a gym to train in. In the winter months it did get cold in the basement. On those cold nights, I dreamed about my life in boxing and where I wanted to be three years from now.

My ultimate goal was to be the heavy weight champion of the world. I had a goal and I knew what and where I wanted to be. I had set my goals high for a teenager who had never even had an amateur fight. I sat down one night and wrote down a plan on how to get to where I wanted to be in five years.

When you decide where you want to go, write it down. When you write it down it is reinforced by:

- Thinking about your goals
- Developing your goals
- Writing down your goals
- Visualize where you want to be
- Reading your goals
- Achieving them

Every one of these steps reinforces your chance of completing your plan. If you write the plan down and read it daily, you are reinforcing your goals.

It becomes your mantra. Read it daily and start to believe it can happen. Never underestimate what you can accomplish if you believe in yourself.

I decided to set my goals high. Do not settle for second best. Rise to the top and become a star performer. I did attain my ambition and goal of being a professional boxer. How do we attain our individual goals? By having a plan!

Buy a Daily Planner

This system works well for me. I recommend you try it. One way to force yourself to complete your short term goals is to buy a daily planner and actually use it. I like the daily and weekly planners that show you the whole week when you open the planner. It gives you a good visual of the week's activity and what you have to do. It will show the entire week from Monday through Sunday.

After you buy your year planner I want you to write down everything you want to get accomplished the first week. This establishes a routine for getting things done. Here is why it will work for you. If you don't get it done that week you have to carry the activity over to the next week or the following week. It's amazing how much you can get done each day if you write down your schedule for that day. Soon you have daily goals that are completed each day. Then you work on weekly, monthly and yearly goals.

Goals Should be Specific and Clear

To be successful you need to set specific and very clear goals. Simplify the goals so they are easily understood and attained. Each day you build on the short term goals. You must be moving forward, sometimes ever so slightly, every day to achieve your vision. For example, my daily goals in preparation to fight for the world heavyweight championship were:

Michael Moorer vs. Evander Holyfield:
Training day 39 of 60 days

- Morning weigh-in: 240 lbs
- Light high carbohydrate breakfast
- 4 mile run in less than 36 minutes
- 200 sit-ups in intervals of 50 (1 minute each set)

- Protein based lunch and nutritional supplements
- Strength training with free weights (back only) and increase weight poundage weekly
- High speed bag (1 minute intervals -10 times)
- 5 rounds of shadow boxing-100 punches thrown per round
- 6 rounds (3 minute rounds) new fighter each round
- Practice jab only-4 rounds
- 20 minutes on the speed bag
- 3 mile speed run (each mile under 8 minutes)
- 50 yard sprints (total of 10)
- Day ends with weigh-in: Target weight of 236 lbs.

If you notice, each day or week I would decrease the running time so I would get in better physical shape. My trainer would increase the weights each week to make me stronger. These are all short-term goals. The plan was at the end of the 60 day training cycle, I would be faster, fitter, lighter and stronger.

All of the dedication and hard work must have worked. I beat Evander Holyfield. That was my second heavyweight championship belt and one of the happiest moments in my life. The trainers and I had a plan. We followed the plan and it worked. Get on a daily plan with short term objectives and just see what happens.

> *Muhammad Ali said this about preparation and training:*
> *"The fight is won or lost far away from witnesses-behind the lines, in the gym, and out there on the road, long before I dance under those lights."*

All Muhammad Ali is saying is that preparation is the key to where you want to be.

If You Fail to Plan, You Plan to Fail

A good friend of mine is a Police Sergeant on the S.W.A.T. Team. He trains the Police Department's S.W.A.T. or Special Weapons and Tactics Team. The S.W.A.T. Team has a mantra and it says, "If you fail to plan, you plan to fail." As a team leader his failure to plan could cost an officer his life. Planning is critical for the S.W.A.T. Team and every operation they go on. He told me that on every call-out the team leader must have a plan in place for anything situation that could occur.

If the barricaded subject starts shooting, the sniper has the green light. If the bad guy refuses to come out, the S.W.A.T. Team goes in and takes him out. What does this mean to you as a leader, everything, because you have to have a solution to every problem. If you don't plan ahead, who will?

Doesn't that make sense to cover all the options? Sometimes a simple plan is better than no plan. Remember, you goals and plans will constantly be changing. You must be flexible but firm. Your goals will need constant revision. Learn to adapt to changes and unforeseen challenges. This will make your company resilient and stronger.

An analogy from boxing would be when my opponent in the ring changes from fighting orthodox to southpaw. What he has done is change his forward foot and his power hand by switching his body. As a boxer I have to adapt to other boxer's new fighting style. I just can't throw my arms up and say, "I quit" because he did something different. If my trainer did his job I would have expected this and trained for it.

Every Day Matters

When you begin your quest for a brighter and better tomorrow, every day is important. You must plan each day and move one inch forward to your goal. Each day you miss, put's you two days behind. It's a lot like building muscle. Either you are working out in the gym building muscle or you are losing muscle by not working out and staying at home. You have to grow every day, not by leaps and bounds but by the inch or centimeter.

As a boxer, I can't miss a day of training. Why? Because I know my next opponent is training to beat me. He is training every day with one goal in mind and that is to beat the world champ. I have the title and he wants it. How bad do you want a bigger house, or a new car or that vacation you always dreamed of? Every day is an important day. Don't waste even a single day. Plan a small part of your day that will take you a little closer to your dream. Does every day really matter? You can bet your life it does. Come to think of it, you are.

> *"You don't get to choose how you're going to die or when. You can only decide how you're going to live now."*

> —*Joan Baez- Singer and Song Writer*

What Joan Baez is saying is that it is your decision on how you want to live your life. Only you can decide how you want to live. You can decide to be famous by writing books or songs or you can become the President of the United States. The only person that controls your life is you. You can be the Champ or the Chump by changing only one letter and that letter is u.

The Sooner the Better

We all know that after reading this book your average 58-year-old male or female isn't going to go to the boxing gym and begin boxing for a living. Here is the scenario. You arrive at the boxing gym and say, "Yeah, I read Michael Moorer's book and here I am, your next heavy-weight champion of the world. We all know that is not going to happen. But what if you wanted to start your own business, quit smoking, go on a diet or find a mate? Now that is possible.

Age can also be an asset. Take for example Ray Kroc. He was the founder of McDonalds. His first restaurant was opened when he was 52 years old. Today there are thousands of McDonald's restaurants in every city in the United States and around the world. Age and experience always complement each other.

Colonel Sanders was 65 when he started Kentucky Fried Chicken. You can work effectively in your later years. You will also discover that most millionaires are still working in their later years. Only 20% of millionaires are retirees. The other 80% still go to work.

Walt Disney filed for bankruptcy 13 times before he accomplished his dream of creating Disneyland and Disneyworld. Did you know that the average millionaire goes bankrupt at least 3.5 times before he/she makes it?

All of these successful men remained motivated and undeterred by their age or limited funds. Motivated people get things done. Success is the product of progress. So the sooner you get started the better.

Do What You Love

I loved beating up other men for a living. Don't make that face because you and the spectators enjoyed it more than I did. Thank God I still have some money from boxing to retire on. My point is I enjoyed boxing for a living.

What about you? When you go to work tomorrow are you excited to get there? Do you enjoy working with your peers and your boss? If you don't have that feeling of enjoyment going to work then I want you to quit your job. Whoa, wait a minute Michael? You want me to quit my job? "Yes, that right, I want you to quit. Not today or tomorrow but soon." I want you to start today and ask yourself what job would complete my life and then start moving in that direction.

If you always wanted to be an artist and paint then go get lessons on how to paint on canvas. There are schools everywhere.

If you wanted to write books or novels then go to night school after work and learn the ins and outs of writing.

Maybe you want to own your own business? Then find out what business you want and start it. The founder of Office Depot started in his garage, so can you!

There are no excuses only your ambition.

Find out what you want to do in life and for the next ten years do nothing but work your way toward that dream. It doesn't matter what your dream is. You can still find some kind of success if you just try.

What you want to be doesn't matter. What matters is you take some kind of action to get to that position one day. Do something every day that brings you closer to that dream and your personal vision. Remember it begins with a dream and then transforms into a vision. With a vision you can see where you want to go. Now it's up to you.

Secret to Success

One of the secrets to success is to do something you love doing. That can be making chocolate candy for your friends at holidays, painting on a canvas or designing web sites. If you truly enjoy what you do, you will never work a day in your life. That's not to say that everything you do, you will love. That is absolutely not true. I love boxing but I really didn't like the 4:00 am road runs in 30 degree Pittsburgh weather, but still I ran each day. It was torture but it was a part of my job as a professional boxer.

Many people are successful and have money, love, fame and expensive jewelry but still they are not happy. Why is this? You can have all the money in the world but if life does not have meaning you will not find happiness.

Look at how many successful actors, actresses, or professional athlete's end up on drugs or kill themselves. They have it all and still they are not happy. Success in life can be measured differently by each person. Finding your own success is more than just fame but an overall package that includes a family, religion, friends, money, being loved, loving someone else and more. The teaching point here is clear. Do something you enjoy. Start a career or business that you love to do. Remember, a skill can always be learned but passion and love come from within.

Change

Trying to change someone else is extremely difficult. Trying to change yourself is not an easy task but it can be done. It all depends on your desire and intensity for the change.

Studies have shown that if you want to change a bad habit it can be accomplished in exactly 21 days. You do the opposite of the bad habit for 21 consecutive days and the change will come naturally and become part of your daily lifestyle.

The secret to making the change permanent is to stay the course for the total 21 days in a row. If you do that you can stop smoking, quit chewing your fingernails and lose that weight you have gained the last few years. At the end of the 21 days the bad habit has been replaced by the good habit. Try it. It has been successful many times.

Firearms and Change

You have to want to change before you can change. I will say it again, "There will be no change unless you want to change." It starts with your perception. If you change the way you think, it will change the way you live.

If you change the way you dress it could change your social environment. Change your hair and people will look at you different. Some changes are easy and some are very difficult. All you have to do is make a small change in your behavior or thinking and the actual results will be just barely measureable at first but after a while will become incredible. Small changes can produce remarkable results.

It is very much like shooting a gun. If you make a small change at the firing line, down range the change is quite significant.

If the barrel of the gun is pointed down range and you are 1/10th of an inch off the target when you pull that trigger the bullet travels down range and completely misses the target. With every foot it travels the angel gets wider and off the normal trajectory path taking you away from the bulls eye. The same thing occurs in life if you make one small change. The longer you continue making the change the more you distance yourself from your past and create new opportunities in your life.

How do we get back on target or get our life back together? All you have to do is make a small change. If we use the firearm analogy again it works. If you move the front sight of the gun just a little, to about a 1/10th of a degree, that small amount at the firing line will now put you right on target.

You will now hit the bulls eye target. Small changes over time or distance create bigger changes. It is exactly the same with your life. Make that change now and you will see the difference in a short period of time.

Agree to make a small change today and see what happens one month or one year from now. That change could be as simple as learning one new word each day and using the new word in a sentence once or twice during the day. That one small change in your vocabulary could change your life dramatically. You will be able to express yourself more clearly and at the same time raising your standard of intelligence.

Let's just examine one more easy change. One change might be to arrive at work ten minutes early. You would be surprised at who will take notice. What does that do for you? First, you are not stressed from the drive or traffic when you get there. Secondly, it shows others and your supervisor that "you care about the company." Three, you have a few minutes to relax, grab a coffee and set your schedule for the day.

As a business owner, when an employee is already at work when I arrive, it makes me take notice. A small change in your behavior can change your life forever. Don't you see the connection? Try it. The change could get you that promotion you have wanted for the past ten years.

The Habit of Winning

Winning as well as losing is a habit. When I boxed professionally, I expected myself to win each fight. There is no second place in boxing. Either you win or you lose. There are no "good loses." I didn't go into a fight to lose. Get in the habit of expecting to win every time.

Once you have changed the way you think you will see remarkable results. You will begin to strive for perfection because that is what produces results. Good results equal a win. Get in the habit of expecting to win and pretty soon you will.

"Impossible is a word to be found only in the dictionary of fools."

—Napoleon Bonaparte

Have a 5 Year, 10 Year and 15 Year Plan

One Christmas I was meeting with a friend of mine to discuss my pre-fight training schedule, I said, "Ward, how about mid June? Does that work for you?" He pulls out his date book and looks at me and says, "What year?" I replied, "What do you mean what year?" He then showed me his planner. This professional trainer had a calendar that took him three years in advance. Talk about planning ahead. He taught me something that Christmas about scheduling and planning ahead. The point to the story is that you have to plan ahead, not one year or two years but three to five years.

Financial Planning

I was one of the lucky boxers who accelerated quickly through the light heavyweight boxing ranks. After winning that division and successfully defending my title several times, I moved to the heavy-weight division. I was always fighting my weight and having trouble keeping the weight off. Every year my body started growing and I put on several pounds of muscle. It was a natural transition to go to the heavyweight division.

For most boxers it is a 10 year plan to get to where you have the opportunity to fight for the heavyweight championship of the world. In the beginning of your boxing career you fight more often because the caliber of your opponent is not that strong. But the higher you get ranked, especially in the top ten; your opponents are all motivated and tough. At this level there are no easy fights.

A boxer fights on the average of three times a year. You will fight more often your first four or five years because you are not fighting the top ranked boxers. After seven or eight years of boxing you hopefully have, a professional record of 30 wins and no loses. So far, this is a 10 year plan to get to the next level.

Up to now, it's been all training and scheduled fights with very little financial reward. Are you willing to sacrifice ten years of your life to your profession? It is a journey to box professionally, open your own restaurant or start your own business? I was in business for almost 10 years before I received a significant paycheck.

Okay, here is the plan. Michael you are going to live with friends, rela-tives, and other trainers, train six hours a day, pay for your own food and make absolutely no money for the first 10 years. After ten 10 years if you haven't lost a fight and you are still healthy, only then, maybe we can make some money. Are you in? I was. Prepare yourself for a long road to success.

The point here is that you should have a financial plan. Whether it is a lot of money or very little money it is all relative. I made millions of dollars and spent millions of dollars. You make $38,000 dollars a year and should have a savings, budget and retirement plan. We all work and receive a pay check. Everyone, every business and every family should have a financial plan that began years ago.

Set Short Term and Attainable Goals

During my boxing career, my short-term goal was to win my next fight. My next goal was to get better and beat a ranked opponent. I wanted to move up to the top 10 ranking of boxers in the world. The competition will get harder the closer you get to the top. But this is also where the money is. This also applies to business. The larger you get, the more difficult it becomes because now you are competing with the big boys.

Set short-term goals. Write them down in your daily planner. Your goal for today could be as simple as buying a set of motivation tapes. Your next goal is to play them while you drive to work. Another short-term goal would be to start reading up on your new career. After a while, short-term goals become bigger and you have to work a little harder to accomplish them. Nevertheless, what is important is that you are now moving in a positive direction and making progress every day.

"The greater danger for most of us is not that our aim is too high and we miss it, but that it is too low and we reach it."

—Michelangelo

Ten Strategies for Success

1. Think Big
Donald Trump has always proffered "thinking big." Don't set your goals to low. Set higher goals that are even bigger than you dreamed of.

2. Choose a Model for Wealth
We don't have to reinvent the wheel. Choose a model of excellence where the road to wealth is already paved. Get on it and make it better.

3. Believe in Yourself
If you don't have the self confidence and believe in your abilities nobody will believe in you. The more self confidence you have the more action you will take.

4. Take Action Everyday
Every day you do not take a positive movement forward you fall back one day to achieving your goals. Make everyday count.

5. Lean, Mean, Fighting Machine

Your health and fitness will determine your energy output. Work on getting in shape. It is time to start taking care of yourself and then your business. You are the drive that makes the business work.

6. Stop Making Excuses

It's time to "man up" whether you are a man or woman. Get rid of any and all excuses. Accept the responsibility. Take positive actions that will increase your chances for success.

7. Get Over Your Fears

The sooner you quit making excuses and face your fears, uncertainties and doubt the faster you begin to make money. If you worked for it, you deserve to be rewarded.

8. Practice the Three "D's."

Discipline, Determination and Drive.

If you combine these three activities together, it will take you further and faster to success than you can ever imagined.

9. Stay Focused on Hi-Value Activities

The more time you invest on hi-value activities the greater return you will have on your investment. Your

time is valuable. Don't waste it. Invest in it wisely.

10. Condition Yourself to Work Longer

Start earlier, finish later and work harder and smarter in between. Condition yourself to be able to perform at a peak performance.

Key Points of Round 2: Have a plan and set goals

- Develop a plan.
- Set short term goals.
- Establish long term goals.
- Buy a daily planner and use it daily.

Progressive Action Steps (PAS)   **Completed**

1. Carry and use your daily planner every day.   ☐

2. Write your goals down.   ☐

3. List 5 PAS things you have to do each day.   ☐

4. Prioritize your goals.   ☐

5. Begin to take action.   ☐

6. Accomplish your daily goals.   ☐

<u>ROUND 3</u>
Take Action

"Well done is better than well said."

—Ben Franklin

Winners Are Action Oriented

You can talk about it as much as you like. You can write it down on five daily planners and on a hundred different progressive charts but nothing get's accomplished until you have taken some kind of action. You have to move in a direction that will complete your objective. It is critical to your success to take action and begin to move forward. It doesn't matter how small the steps are but what is important is you are taking some kind of action in a positive direction.

In your life you can sit down and watch what happens around you or you can get up and get involved. Don't be a spectator in life become a person that gets it done. Don't let it happen, make it happen. When you decide to make it happen you have some control over the outcome, otherwise it is a turkey shoot. Winners are action oriented.

Winners decide on a course of action and start moving in that direction. They make their mind up and set short term achievable goals. What separates them from the others is that makes winners is they decide on a course of action and then act. Losers dwell on the problem and then do nothing.

What separates the winners from the losers? History will show you that it is not the genius concepts or great ideas, but the implementation and execution of those concepts and ideas.

Take Action Every Day

A lot of people are on life's treadmill. They are working like hell but just not getting anywhere. Why is that? It is because they are not moving in the right direction. Yes, they are moving but in what direction? This person has no daily objectives, no goals or new challenges. They do the same thing every day and then they wonder why they are not getting ahead in life.

You must force yourself each day to move in the direction of your dreams. If you want to paint portraits then what do you have to do? Step one may be to start saving for an easel, brushes and oil paint. After a month you can afford to go out and buy the supplies. But, in the meantime you could start pencil sketching every person you see. Do you get the progressive action point?

Every day do something (activity or action) that gets you one-step closer to your vision. Do it now. To succeed you must be committed. Commitment combined with action equals results.

> *The great golfer Ben Hogan said it best: "As you walk down the fairway of life, you must smell the roses, for you only get to play one round."*

What this quote means is that you have to find a balance between working hard and sharing time with your family and yourself. Enjoy life because you only get one chance at it. Don't waste your opportunity on this earth to be somebody. We only have one life, live it well.

I know that many of the people who read this book are most likely working full time, maybe you have a couple children and you are absolutely exhausted when you get home from work.

I understand that but, if you want that dream to come true, then you have to get up off the couch and do something to better your life and your standard of living. There is always that adage about being overweight, "How is it that people who can never find time to exercise but can always find time to eat? Remember, goals are nothing without action. Find the time, make the time to take action and achieve your dreams.

President John F. Kennedy told this story during a military briefing. The story is about taking action.

"The great French Marshall Lyautey once asked his gardener to plant a tree. The gardener objected that the tree was slow growing and would not reach maturity for 100 years. That's when Marshall Lyautey replied, "In that case, there is no time to lose; plant it this afternoon."

Training

When I first started out as a boxer, I didn't know a left jab from an upper cut. But, I had passion for the sport and I knew what I wanted to do with my life. I wanted to fight for a living. Do you know even today I have never had a full time job?

So I decided early in my life what I wanted to do. The only problem was that I had very few or no boxing skills at all. What I did have was lots of inspiration and desire. I knew the sacrifices, time line and chances of making it big were slim. I still chose boxing as my career choice.

Growing up I wasn't your chiseled muscular fighter. In fact, I wasn't even that big. I was tall and very lean. The chance of me making it to the top ten ranked boxers was not very good. I didn't care. As a youth I knew what I wanted in my life. I went to the gym with my grandfather and he taught me the boxing business.

I learned that boxing is more than just a sport. It is a business that includes a lot of good things and some bad. It's a lot like the duck swimming on the pond. In the water the duck looks collected, calm and in control. But underneath the water those little legs and web feet are going a hundred miles an hour. Not everything is what you see on the surface. That's another story about boxing behind the ropes.

If your goal is to one day own a restaurant then go work in a restaurant. Learn the skills of running a restaurant and how to manage a food establishment. You may have to start waiting on tables. Then after you have waited on tables for one year someone asks you to cook. As the cook you will learn how to prepare meals, season certain foods and unload the food truck. Now, after being in the business for four years you are asked to be the assistant manager.

As a manager you will learn a different skill set. Managers have to know what sells, what to order, profit and loss, purchasing food and how to hire, fire and manage employees. Now, after seven years you know the restaurant business. You have done it all from the ground floor up.

During the past seven years you gained valuable experience. You started at the bottom and learned every position from waiter, cook to manager. After seven years and doing just about every job in the restaurant business, only now should you consider opening your own restaurant.

Now comes the question? Do I take all of my savings and open a restaurant of my own? I will be risking everything I own. I have the idea making the restaurant look like a police station. memorabilia and guns on the walls, every table has a police scanner, employees dress in law enforcement uniforms, etc.

My dilemma is, do I play it safe and continue being the manager where I work or do I open my own restaurant?

"A ship in port is safe, but that is not what ships are built for."

—Benazir Bhutto- Prime Minister of Pakistan

The Great White Hope

A friend of mine, Eddie, was a police officer. He wanted to own his own restaurant but knew nothing about the restaurant business. He told me, I will hire the best managers, the best cooks and the most experienced waitresses to run the place. Eddie also said, "I don't need to have experience, I will hire it." So Eddie borrows money on his house and from the credit union and opens up a Cuban restaurant in a shopping plaza.

After one week I go there to eat and to support my friend's new venture. He's there working. He's waiting on tables, helping in the kitchen and taking cash. After a fair meal, (the food wasn't that great) I asked Eddie, "Congratulations, on opening the restaurant, how is it going?" He replied, "It's a project in the making but I'm working on it."

After just six weeks the restaurant was running out of money and Eddie wanted out. He was not cut out to be a restaurant manager or owner.

The lesson here is, you can't take a pig and make him produce milk. In the boxing business I see it every day. Former football players with athletic skills can't make it in football so they decide to become professional boxers. That's Eddie the police officer trying to become a restaurant owner.

Several years ago I was assisting at a local boxing gym. Most of the "boxers" were former football players and thought they could box because they played football in college.

We get the "Great White Hope" who thinks he is going to be the next Rocky Marciano. I did my best with them but they believed the business of boxing was easy. It is not. Most of them lose their first fight and move on to MMA, quit or try something else. I fought over 70 times as an amateur before I got my first paycheck.

Here is the point of the story. In business, boxing or sales you have to pay your dues and be realistic about your goals. It takes action, planning and sometimes years to get to where you want to be. You will work hard and put in long hours. But, if you stick with it and you have no fear, you just might be able to be somebody someday.

Did you ever think we would have a black man as the President of the United States? I never thought there would be a brown man as the President during my lifetime. You don't think Barack Obama had concerns and fears about even running for office and if he actually won? Of course he did. He believed he could do it and history tells the rest of the story. There is opportunity for everyone. Just go out and try.

> *"Often the difference between a successful man and a failure is not one's abilities or ideas, but the courage that one has to bet on his ideas, to take a calculated risk – and to act."*
>
> *—Maxwell Maltz*

Winners Take Risks

To be a winner, you have to take risks. Sometimes the reward outweighs the risks. You or your company will never grow if you just stand still. You have to take calculated risks to succeed. Several times in my career I took a fight that was risky. Boxing journalists wrote that I wasn't ready; the fighter was too big, too fast or just too experienced. I listened to my managers and trainers and many times they would say, "Michael, it's up to you, it's your decision." I looked at all the facts and only then would I make the decision.

If you do your due diligence and have all the facts, the answer becomes a little more clearer. That is when you, the business owner, the professional, have to make the decision. You have to weigh all of the options and decide what is best for you, your family and your company. You also have to think about what if I lose? If you lose, how will that affect the organization, but if you win, where will you be next year?

As a boxer, if I win I get to fight in the top ten and maybe a chance for the championship. But, if I lose it is a mark on my record that will never go away. Every boxer hates that first loss. It is important that you weigh all the odds and listen to your gut feeling before taking that risk and making your decision.

"I find the great thing in this world is not so much where we stand as in what direction we are moving."

—Oliver Wendell Holmes

Making a Difference

This is a story about how one person can make a difference in someone's life.

Early one morning, an old man was standing on the beach and was undecided what to do. After a few minutes he made his mind up and he knew exactly what he had to do. He started making a difference.

During the night, thousands of starfish had washed up onto the beach and they were dying. He was throwing them back into the ocean. The man was weak and very old. Each time he bent over to pick up a star fish took just a little more energy from the old man but he kept doing it. He didn't stop. He would bend over slowly and gently pick up the next starfish and throw it back into the ocean. The old man was getting tired. Even though he was tired he kept throwing them back into the ocean. The beach was covered with starfish. You could hardly take a step without finding another dying starfish.

A young man approached him on the beach and asked him what he was doing. The old man replied, "I'm making a difference." The young man looked around at all the dying starfish and laughed. He then looked at the old man and said, "A difference. There are probably a million starfish on this beach, you can't possibly think you are making a difference." The old man picked up another starfish and said, "It makes a difference to this one" and threw it back into the sea."

You can make a difference in your life or another person's life. Make a difference in your lifetime, even if it is only one starfish.

Start Thinking Positive

If you want to change your life, you have to change the way you think. Studies have shown that you become what you think about. So, how do I improve my life? The answer is changing your environment. It is time to surround yourself with friends and associates that are all achievers. These people are winners and are always moving forward and constantly entertain positive thoughts and not negative. You are what you eat and you become what you think.

From now on don't associate or hang around people who are negative. They will drain the inspiration from you and leave you deflated. Remember the quote, "Misery loves company." If you continue to befriend and socialize with people who are negative, it will short-circuit your production.

As a professional boxer and trying to move up in the rankings, I needed to train with the best talent. Do I want to spar and train with some slug who is paid $15.00 an hour to spar with me or an up and coming boxer that will push me past my limits and make me better? Of course, I want the up and coming boxer that will push my limits. It is the same thing with your training partners. Find a new set of friends who are on the way up. That is exactly what some of my training partners did. They saw I was moving up the chart and getting better fights. They got better by sparing and working with me. A positive attitude benefits everyone.

Start filling your mental template with positive input. One motivational speaker talks about how he would begin his day. He would read the morning paper. The newspaper was filled with domestic crisis, murders, traffic accidents, deaths, shootings, stabbings, rapes, financial losses and then he would go to work and what, try being positive. That is not a good way to start your day. Think only good things and start believing in yourself. Recognize the fact that you have purpose in this life and start believing things will get better.

"We must either find a way or make one."

—Hannibal

The Corn Farmer

When a farmer plants corn seed in the ground, what do you think will grow out of the seeded ground? It will be corn. It is the same analogy for you. If you put negative thoughts in your brain, what are you going to be thinking about?

What are you putting or planting in your brain every day? What is the result; exactly what you put in there. If you plant corn, you get corn. If you plant positive thoughts, goals and inspirations, you start to think of what you can do rather than what you cannot accomplish. Positive thoughts evoke positive outcome.

"It is better to light one small candle than to curse the darkness."

—Confucius

What Confucius is saying is do something rather than just sit there and do nothing.

Key Points of Round 3: Take Action

- Winners are action oriented
- Start changing your life today
- Take positive action everyday
- Start believing in yourself
- Feed your brain positive information and not negative

Progressive Action Steps (PAS)　　Completed

1. I have found new friends who are positive.　□

2. I bought a book/tape on motivation.　□

3. I have a plan and today I took action.　□

4. I worked hard today and paid my dues　□

Notes

ROUND 4
Build your skills

"I visualized where I wanted to be, what kind of a player I wanted to become. I knew exactly where I wanted to go, and I focused on getting there."

—*Michael Jordan*

Michael Moorer's Boxing History

I still think about coming out of retirement and boxing again. I do miss the competition, the training and the physical combat between two warriors. If you have ever seen anyone of my fights, before the bell rings I am usually very calm. To me it's all business. I don't yell across the ring or make unrealistic predictions. I'm there to take care of business. Even after I win, I'm still the calm collected Double "M." That was my nickname as a boxer.

I'm not that type of person that brags about himself. People have said that I am a soft-spoken man. I would say that is true. Reporters have claimed I have a menacing stare. I would say this is also true. I was one of the more fortunate professional boxers in that I won the Lightweight Championship my 11th pro fight. I was 20 years old and on top of the world.

Before any fight I am in a zone. You could fire a gun next to my head and I wouldn't flinch. Did you ever watch National Geographic when they studied the lions in Africa? The camera would capture the lions fixed stare as they stalked their prey. The animal's concentration was incredible. That's me. I guess that is where the sports writers wrote about my menacing stare.

Before a championship fight I don't get excited. I kind of go into a zone and all I think about is what I'm going to do when the fight starts. You could say I do my talking in the ring with my fists. I was gifted with the ability to punch. Not only punch somebody but rock their entire body when I hit them. That was one of my best boxing skills.

I think it is important that you know where I came from and a little bit about my amateur boxing career.

I was born in Brooklyn, New York on November 12, 1967. I moved to Monessen, Pennsylvania a few years later. That is where I grew up and learned how to box. My grandfather, Henry Smith, raised me. He was a boxer in the 1940's. He taught me the art of boxing.

Every day after school I would have house chores and yard work. My grandfather would leave me alone everyday and go to the boxing gym. One day I worked really fast and extra hard and finished everything before he left. When he was just about to leave I asked him if I could go with him and he said, "Yes." That day changed my life forever. I was 10 years old and going to the boxing gym for the first time.

When we got there my grandfather was busy with the other boxers and I just walked around in the boxing gym. He had the nickname of "Superman." That is what everyone called him. The boxing gym in Charleroi wasn't anything fancy but it served our purpose for my development as a boxer.

My very first day in the gym, I just went over to one of the hanging heavy bags and started hitting it with my closed first. Superman looked over in amazement.

When novice boxers hit the heavy bag you usually hear a pop. A combination would sound like Pop, pop, and pop. When I started hitting the bag my grandfather took notice. When I hit the bag it made a thud sound and not a pop. I guess I was born with punching power.

The Amateur Years

In 1985, I was the runner up at the ABF Nationals. In 1986 I won the United States Amateur Light Middleweight championship. I was tall but needed to fill out a little bit before I would fight for the heavy-weight title. I was skinny and still building my boxing skills.

My amateur record was 48 wins and 16 losses. After a string of consecutive wins with no loses I decided to turn pro. That is when I moved into a room in the basement of my trainer Emanuel Steward. My first pro fight was when I was 18 years old. I fought Adrian Riggs on March 4, 1988. I KO'd him in the first round. All my hard work and determination paid off. I got my first win as a professional and my first knockout. It was a good night.

After that, I went on to win my next 21 fights knocking out all of my opponents. In 1988, I won the WBO light heavyweight title by knocking out Ramzi Hassan in the 5th round. I went on to defend the title nine times before I moved up to a higher weight class. In 1991, I won my first world heavyweight championship title when I knocked out Bert Cooper in the fifth round. I was 24 years old and the Heavyweight Champion of the World.

So, there is the story, now here is the teaching point. I fought as an amateur 64 times. I had a few loses but each time I would learn from my defeat. With every fight, I was building my skills. That was eight years of boxing education before I fought my first professional fight.

What does that mean to you? To be a champion or winner in life takes time, your time and your personal sacrifice. I was working part-time during my amateur years while I was building my skills. In boxing, business or a trade profession, it takes years to become good at what you do.

When you finally make that decision to change and choose a profession, be prepared to get knocked down. It will not be easy. Doors will close and some will open but plan on some difficult days (that's my 16 loses as an amateur) and after taking the hits you have to get right back up and continue on your path to success. How many other boxers would have quit after being beaten 16 times as an amateur? I didn't.

The most famous basketball player of all time, Michael Jordan said, "I can accept failure, everyone fails at something. But I can't accept not trying."

Determination and Skill

I have often been asked what made me a successful pugilist or professional boxer. I believe it was my intense desire not to lose. I just didn't like losing. The more I lost the more I trained. You have to ask yourself what will get me to the top? I may have the skill but I need one more thing. Here is some good advice. If you are going to do it, do it right and don't fudge. Your determination will determine your success.

What made me the world champion? What pushed George Foreman to leave being a minister and start boxing again? It was and still is your determination and skill. Anyone can be determined but you have to match that with a skill. Your skill could be a carpenter, an artist, songwriter or even a rodeo cowboy. You can't be successful unless you combine your skill with a determination not to quit.

Your Style is Important

Sometimes it's not your skill, but the way you deliver it. What I mean is that after beating Holyfield, I fought George Foreman. He is an orthodox style boxer and I am a southpaw. I thought Foreman's style fit me perfectly. George was much older than me and being in his mid forties a little slower throwing and deflecting punches. I thought I could beat him. I had no doubt I could knock him out if I could just stay outside of his left foot.

I believed that until he hit me with a straight right hand or it might have been one of his George Foreman lean mean cooking grills, I couldn't tell. I thought I could beat him. Well you know that didn't happen. His right hand put me down.

But, sometimes you possess all the skills in the world but your delivery style doesn't work. Some football teams always beat another team all the time. It's style, not technique or skill that can give you the edge.

My point here is you may be the most talented person in your field, but if you can't match the style of your audience, opponent or boss you will never win.

It's like a comedian that goes around the country on a comic circuit. Do you think he uses the same jokes and profanity in the Deep South that he would use in New York City or Las Vegas? The cultures are different which require a different style of comedy.

Education or Training

It is a proven fact that anyone who goes to school and get's an education makes more money than the uneducated worker. Football players, boxers and starting your own business do not require a high school education or a college degree. But it does help in every field.

I became proficient in boxing by on the job experience. I went to the gym every day and worked on my skills. That was my education. To be good at boxing or any skill takes years and thousands of hours on the job. Did you ever see a really skilled carpenter? That carpenter didn't just pick up a skill saw and make a dresser out of a bunch of wood. Hopefully you are good at what you do but you really won't know until you put years into the business or sport.

To be good, put in the time. In business or your trade, you may have learned the skills of being a roofer or a cook in a restaurant. After eight years, you and a few friends decide to open your own roofing company or restaurant. The only problem is that you know how to only put shingle down or repair a roof. That's great but your business and or office skills are minimal. You have no training in accounting, computer skills or writing a proposal.

What's the answer? The answer is you need both. You have to manage your time and get that education to run the office and at the same time hone your skills as a roofer or athlete. It's important what you do on the field and off the field. As a boxer I fought and at the same time did get some education on finances and running a business.

Many of my friends who are professional athletes do nothing but train in the sport they have chosen. It is there full time job. They would train, train and train some more. Finally, they made it to the big league. They thought the money would be enough to carry them through their entire life. Usually it is not. The money runs out and they have absolutely no life skills. They are or were great athletes but are lousy at math. Now what do they do?

Success is a multi package deal. Yes, you can work hard, gain fame, and make lots of money. But, you have to have the education and knowledge to invest your money and plan for your future after boxing or your career. We all have stages in our lives and need to plan for each one. So, the answer is you have to train for your profession and at the same time learn life skills to manage your success.

Leadership and Team Building Through Sports

If you want to build your leadership and team building skills get involved in a competitive organized team sport. Numerous studies have shown that individuals who play sports become better business professionals and CEO's of companies.

When you are involved in sports it builds your competitive spirit. You learn to like winning and the agony of losing. What is that saying, "Show me a good loser and I will show you a loser?" You don't set team and individual goals to lose. Your team sets goals to win. As an individual on a team you train hard to achieve those goals as a team. Soon you lose your individuality and become a team member.

As a team member you learn to interact with others. It doesn't matter whether you are the team leader or a team member. It becomes a common goal for the group to win. As a team leader you delegate duties and follow-up to make sure your team mate is performing his or her responsibilities. You develop team-building skills by working together for a common cause.

Competition in any sport is pressure. Whether it is a team sport or an individual sport you learn how to deal with the pressure of winning or losing. It all comes down to getting that last yard in football, you need that hit in baseball or blocking that volley ball back to the other side of the net. There will be pressure and stress in becoming successful or playing a competitive sport. You can learn to deal with the pressure by playing sports. Sports is a game, where making the wrong decision in business could bankrupt your company. You will learn to make decisive decisions that could affect you for the rest of your life.

Playing sports teaches you how to be competitive in life. It's funny, but if you look at life, it is all about competition. We try to make more money than our friends. I lose weight so I can get that girl. I want to be the CEO of my own company so I won't have to take orders from anyone. If you are not competitive, you will end up being a follower rather than a leader. Does that statement make you mad? I hope so. If it does, welcome to your first step in becoming successful.

Focus

Learning how to focus is a skill that takes time to master. All of the winning pros have it. Professional tennis players will say, "The tennis ball looked like a grapefruit today." That is focus. Everyone needs to learn how to focus. It doesn't matter if you are an actor, singer, hockey player, or CEO, learning how to focus is a learned skill.

On all of my fights, I would slowly begin focusing on the match about three or four hours prior to getting into the ring. An hour or two before the bell would ring; I would be in a zone. I was concentrating on the fight. I would visualize myself knocking out my opponent. My focus would be so intense that one of my trainers commented, "He scares me. His concentration is so intense I would hate to be the guy he is fighting." During the fight I was in a zone and focused where I could see the punch coming before it got to me.

If you have an audition for a big part in a movie or you are the guest speaker at the Oscar's, find a quiet place and be by yourself. Shut out distractions for just a few minutes. Focus and concentrate on what you have to do. See yourself doing it, practice saying it and visualize it. When you walk out to begin your performance, you will be incredible. You are now the entrepreneurial athlete.

Achieving Your Potential

Much like a professional boxer, successful people are a "work in progress." Just like boxing skills, you don't acquire business skills overnight. The necessary skills to be successful take years to develop. Therefore, you must be patient. Set aside those plans to conquer the world before lunch. I started my 30 year boxing journey at the age of 10 years old.

Look at the Olympic Games. Every four years world class athletes beat world records from the previous year. Olympic runners and swimmers achieve their personal best times and then beat that time weeks later.

We can all improve and become better. Try daily self improvement. Enhance your skill set daily by learning a new word, becoming a better leader or perfecting a physical skill every day of your life. Let's all try to be better and achieve our personal potential every day.

Put the Time In

Education and training is important to every profession. As a boxer, I receive most of my education in the gym and the ring. I ran thousands of miles in preparation for my fights. You have to put the time in if you want success.

If you want to be the best chef in the world you should read hundreds of books on cooking, go to culinary school and then put in ten years as a cook or chef in a restaurant. Now, maybe you are ready.

You have got to put in the time. Don't rush it. If you are an actor trying out for a new part and you have not prepared yourself, you will not get the part. If you try out for American Idol and you don't make it to Hollywood, you either have no talent or have not put in the time. In some careers it is your God given talent and time that takes you to the top. Some people have it and some don't. I guess that is why I wasn't a professional singer.

I never took a fight where I thought I was not ready. I had lots of talent and put in thousands of hours honing my skills to be a better boxer. You have to do the same. It doesn't matter if you are a salesperson, teacher, an actor or an artist. You have to sacrifice and put in the hours, time and effort. It's call sacrifice.

Talent and Skill

Some careers are all or nothing. What does that mean? The difference is talent and skill. Both can be acquired to a certain point but only one is a gift that is inherent in only a few people. The other is acquired by repetition. Of the two, skill or talent, which is more important? The answer is talent.

I can take anyone and teach them the basic skills to cut down trees, play baseball, or paint on a canvas. That is an acquired skill. You can be very good at these skills but only through years of practice do you get better.

What I can't teach someone is talent. Talent to sing, act or box professionally. Either you have it or you don't. This is where you see boxers with records of 35 fights with 20 defeats or actors who get small parts but just can't land the big roles.

What's my point? When you decide on a new career, be realistic. Ask yourself, "Do you have a talent or a skill to get to where you want to go?" In my professional boxing record I have had four loses. Each loss was critical to my career.

I had the talent and the skills but maybe I didn't have the correct strategy for the fights I lost. Of the matches I lost, I really don't think any of the boxers had more talent than I had. Sometimes in boxing you should have ducked rather than weaved and that my friend decides that fight. Remember, the higher you get to the top, the tougher the competition. So choose your future carefully.

John Wright is one Michael Moorer's closes friends. He grew up with Michael through high school and the early years of his boxing career. John was his strength coach and mentor. He said, "You could tell from Michael's first year in boxing that this is what he was destined to do."

Preparation Meets Opportunity

How bad do you want it? Are you willing to sacrifice your family, friends, vacations, standard of living, your education and more to achieve your goal? It just may take all that and more. To get to the top takes extreme sacrifices personally, socially, and economically.

If you sincerely want to achieve something in your lifetime, you have to prepare yourself and be ready when the opportunity arrives. When preparation meets opportunity that is when you have to perform. Are you ready? There are no quick fixes or get rich fast schools of business or avenues of success. It is the school of hard knocks and preparation. You will find out several years from now, the longer the preparation, the greater the reward.

Let's talk about that last line. The longer you prepare and sacrifice the greater the reward. The more time and energy you spend in preparation gives you a better chance of success. Thus you should make more money in your lifetime. This is a proven fact.

Let's not kid ourselves here. I boxed to make the big money. Yes, I loved the sport but I also liked the money. During my professional career it is reported I made 22 million dollars. I wish I knew where it is. You are reading this book for self improvement that may bring you financial, social or happiness. We all seek different goals in life.

"I'm not much of a golfer, I don't have any friends. All I do the day of a game is go home and be alone and worry about ways not to lose."

—Alabama Football Great: Coach Bear Bryant

KSA's: Knowledge, Skills and Abilities

The KSA's are the Knowledge, Skill and Ability to perform. When you begin to learn your new chosen field, the KSA's are the foundation for your success. First, you learn everything you can about becoming an actor, being an electrician or harvesting corn. Next, you acquire the technical and physical skills of doing the job. Work for your neighbor for free or go to school. Lastly, can you apply your knowledge and skills and do something (abilities) with what you have learned. Do you have the ability to succeed or do you need more experience?

Practice Makes Perfect

If you ever attend a professional sporting event such as golf or tennis tournament, I want you to get there early. Why, because you will see the professional golfers and tennis players practicing that morning. They are practicing the morning of the tournament. After playing golf or tennis for 20 years, 6 hours a day, what are the pros doing the day of the tournament? They are on the green or the tennis court perfecting their skills. Like they say, "Practice makes perfect." What does that tell you about being successful?

Good Habits

Humans are creatures of habit. Once you do it enough times the action becomes engrained within your daily activities. To perfect an athletic move it takes 5,000 repetitions for muscle memory to kick in. If you want to change, it will take some work and time.

If you do the same thing over and over again it becomes muscle memory. Your body is trained to perform the same movement by doing multiple repetitions. This includes good habits and bad habits.

Then why not develop good habits rather than bad habits? So, why don't we practice some good business habits? Some techniques that may help contribute to your success would be:

- Good eye contact when you shake hands with someone
- Stand up straight, don't slouch over
- Check yourself for bad breath-good hygiene
- Get a new haircut that reflects your style

- Start looking at everything in a positive way
- Stop chewing your finger nails
- Make <u>everyone</u> you meet feel important
- Dress professional at all times and not part of the time
- Be early rather than being on time or late once in a while
- Where you eat regularly, increase the tip
- Stay after work and improve on current projects
- Recognize good work and acknowledge it (even if you are not a supervisor.)
- Lose some weight
- Become a good listener-actually listen to what other people say
- Wear a good pair of shoes and a nice watch
- Increase your vocabulary
- Stop criticizing other people
- Stop complaining and do something about the problem
- Be authentic. Give honest and sincere answers
- Go find a success group
- Establish new friends that are successful

These are just a few things that will enhance you business etiquette and take you closer to the top. These are some of the small things you can do. Pick one and try it for thirty (30) days. See what happens. It just might be that small action that separates you from the pack. One small change could be the key to your success.

Change Can Be Easy

You don't have to be a fashion model to dress for success. Recently I remodeled my home. I bought five magazines that featured different types of the interiors of houses. I went through the magazines and circled what I wanted in my house. I like the colonial windows, open style kitchen, granite tops and several other designs. I circled them and gave them to my architect. It was that simple.

If you want to dress for success go out and buy a few men's magazines. Thumb through the magazine and circle the outfits that you like and then go out and buy them. The interior designs and clothes for models are proven and tested. Change the way you live by the way you look.

Men and women notice different things about people. A man looks at a woman's body first and then the face. Women and men look at the shoes the man is wearing and then his watch. Remember, first impressions are lasting impressions.

"Do you suppose I could buy back my introduction to you?"

—Groucho Marx

Bad Habits

Ask a close friend to tell you if he or she notices any bad habits that you may have. Ask them to be honest with you and be a friend and tell you the truth. What do you do that irritates them or bothers them? Ask them to be brutally honest. Everyone should be trying to improve themselves for advancement. This is done on a regular basis by actors and professional athletes. Everyone is trying to get just a little bit better so they can move on to the next level.

If you watch some boxers they do the same thing all the time. Bam, bam, they throw a left right combination. Step back, drop their hands and pull their boxing shorts up. It's like a routine. That's when I'm moving in and knocking him out. Bad habits are not good habits.

In this chapter, we are working on building and improving your skills. Are your personal skills good? How do you know? You may think the way you act and perform is good but in reality, you may be lacking in several areas. When politicians run for office they have a coach for everything. The political party will spend tens of thousands of dollars coaching the candidate.

The politician is taught how to shake hands, speak in public, dress, answer questions, look good on camera, dinner etiquette and more. So don't be afraid to ask someone you trust for advice.

Expect Success

You are who you think you are. I will repeat that. You are who you think you are. You have got to start believing in yourself and believe that your life is going to change. You must be patient, work hard, be positive and expect success. It is a state of mind. Stay motivated and expect success and it will come. Psychologists have proven that what you think about actually happens.

It is important to stay focused. In an arena full of screaming fight fans they can cause a momentary lapse in your focus and that's all your opponent needs. He will hit you with a left hook and end your evening. Do not let distractions, no matter how loud, how sexy, or how promising distract you. Don't lose focus and let outside forces get in the way of your personal plan.

Your passion is fueled by an inspiration and you will accomplish your goals if you just keep doing the right thing. Do not deviate from your road to success. Stay focused and at the end of the fight, like me, expect to be standing as the victor.

> *Eleanor Roosevelt said it best- "No one can make you feel inferior without your consent."*

Integrity

Integrity is something you earn from your peers and competitors. It is an admired personal trait that is instilled within you. Integrity takes years to acquire and can be lost in one second. You can destroy it with one devious action or one miss quote or statement. It has tumbled world leaders and U. S. Presidents. When you have integrity, it is something you want to keep and make it stronger every day.

For years motivational teams have studied successful people. What makes this person a great leader? Why is she so successful? What single trait separates this leader and successful person from all the others? The one common denominator in every successful person is integrity. You must maintain a high level of integrity and self-discipline if you want success.

What is integrity? Integrity is that internal policing agent that keeps you heading in the right direction. It is always doing the right thing. Integrity must be maintained throughout your career. Don't lose it for one momentary mistake. It becomes a way of life. Integrity is what you do when no one is watching. Integrity is a lifestyle not a moment to moment decision.

Education the Easy Way

If your schedule is so hectic that you can't attend daily or weekly training classes or you don't have time to enroll in college, then here is the best alternative. I want you to read books. You can pick up books fairly inexpensive today or even better yet go on the internet. It is loaded with training information. You can find anything you want on thousands of topics and careers. There are no excuses now. You can go online or read from your phone.

What I found most rewarding and easy learning is to play motivational and success tapes while driving in my car. Try it and see what happens in your life. Turn the car radio off and get an education everyday on your way to work. The success tapes are inexpensive. Play them more than one time and acquire an education on your way to and from work every day.

Training is important for everyone from the corporate president down to the line worker. Surveys have shown that in corporate America 70% of the large companies train their executives? But in contrast those same companies only train 25% of their line production staff or sales personnel.

It is the company that trains their staff that will be on the cutting edge of technology. Whether you know it or not, technology runs the business world. Always try to be head of the curve. Training and education is a must for all rising executives.

Don't Stay in the Comfort Zone

To gain any kind of progress you have to push yourself to the next level. This is a standard for Olympic athletes. They reach a certain level that is higher than before and they immediately push themselves to the next level. The minute you start feeling comfortable, it's time to move forward. If you stay in your comfort zone you will limit your growth potential. Never stop pushing yourself to learn more and get to the next level.

This same principle applies to lifting weights. If you lift the same amount of weight every day, your body will be accustomed to the weights and after a while will simply stop growing. You will maintain the same size and in some cases loose muscle.

It is not until you start increasing the weights that your body feels a difference and begins to change. The heavier weights begin to feel uncomfortable which forces your body to grow and your muscles begin to get larger. You have to push yourself for peak performance and personal growth.

The SWAT Team

The co-author of this book, Walter Philbrick, was a SWAT Team Leader on his police department. Being on the SWAT Team meant that you were the best of the best. When the patrol officers needed help, they called out the SWAT Team. Just some of the calls the SWAT Team would respond to would be; a barricaded subject, hostage rescue, police officer down, multiple firearms/shooters, and serving arrest warrants for homicide subjects, robbery and narcotics.

Sgt. Philbrick was the SWAT Training Coordinator. He wanted every SWAT Officer to be a crack shot with their handgun, shotgun, MP-5 Machine Gun and the AR-15 M-4 rifle. So, what he and the Lieutenant did was they raised the scores for qualifications on all four weapons. They raised the qualification score for S.W.A.T. from 80% to 90% to qualify. To remain on the S.W.A.T. Team you had to shoot 90% or better. Still the patrol officers could qualify with an 80% but not the SWAT Team members. He expected more from the SWAT Team than individual officers.

After the SWAT Team supervisor raised the bar, several of the team members said, "I will never score a 90% every time, it's just too difficult." Philbrick and the Lieutenant told all the team members, "If you don't qualify with a 90% firearms score or better you are off the team until you do."

What the team supervisors did was push the team members to become better shots. Every man on the team was challenged to perform at a higher level than his comfort zone. Now, they just couldn't qualify. They had to be extremely proficient with not one but all four weapons. Several of the team members expressed concern on not being able to qualify.

Do you want to know what happened? Every member of the SWAT team increased their individual firearm skills and scores. All of the team members passed with 90% or better. Why, because they were required to perform at a higher level. Each team member became better at what they do, because they had to.

What does the story mean to you and me? If you want to achieve anything in this life, you have to push yourself to limits you thought were unattainable. You have to put yourself in that uncomfortable zone. This is an area where you are not sure of yourself. You may have self doubt if you can really get to the next level.

This is where your confidence increases as you rise to meet the challenge. You have to do it, there is no other choice. You will and must push your way through this part of your life. It is the only way to get better.

It is now that time in your life to step up. Quit making excuses for not being where you want to be. Overcome the excuses and for the men and women, "Man up." If you want to be on top of the food chain you are going to have to step up, believe in yourself and sacrifice.

This will take great courage on our part. It will take a strong inner self to take that second job and get up at 5:00 AM every morning and go to work. It will take sacrificing to put every dime you have in your dream to create a better future for you and your family. It will take all the strength and fortitude you have to step out of your comfort zone. It's time to jump to the next level. If you are feeling comfortable, it's time to move forward and challenge yourself to get more out of life. I know it's tough, but you deserve better.

Product Diversity

Do think I could make a living as a professional boxer if I just threw one type of punch. The fight commentator would say something like, "Michael Moorer throws the left hook, and he throws it again. There it is that left hook again. And Michael Moorer hits him with that left hand again. Would I win the fight? Of course not, I would lose the fight. I have to offer more than just one punch. The left hook may be my bread and butter punch but I wouldn't win many fights.

To be successful you have to have one good product that is your staple and at the same time offer the consumer several other products or services. Don't be a one punch fighter.

What you will find out through trial and error is what works for you. After failing 8 or 9 times you will make the adjustment and find the right service or product. Do not quit. Remember failure is not terminal it's just a chance to start over and do it better. If you hang in there, you can make it happen.

The Psychology of Winning

To be successful you have got to program yourself much like a computer. Think of your brain as a data base or a computer chip. What you put in or feed your brain is stored there and ready when you want it back. Did you ever hear the saying, "garbage in, garbage out?" Maybe it's time we started to feed our brain differently. If you think negative thoughts, you will only get negative responses. We become what we think about most. You will reap the seeds you sew.

So if you want to succeed, start programming yourself now for progressive thoughts. You have to start believing that you can do it. Think only positive thoughts and only take actions that will increase your chances for success. Listen to motivational tapes, join book clubs, and read books on how to be successful and win. Start programming yourself to be a winner. Slowly at first and then accelerate when you feel confident. You have to start now, today.

> *Winston Churchill said, "Success is not final, failure is not fatal, it is the courage to continue that counts."*

Study Your Competition

Much like any business or sporting event, you have to study your competition. Before every fight, I would gather as much information I could find on my opponent and study his movements and boxing patterns. It is the same in business. If you fail to prepare yourself for the competition, your company's chance of success will be limited.

Look what happened to Iron Mike Tyson when he fought Buster Douglas in Tokyo, Japan on February 11, 1990. Tyson was the heavyweight boxing champion of the world and had a record of 42 wins and no loses. He knocked out the majority of his fighters in the first few rounds.

Tyson was technically the better boxer but he did not properly prepare himself for Buster Douglas. Iron Mike Tyson with an undefeated record got knocked out. That was the end of a legend. That one defeat in an incredible career had more affect on his life than all the victories before that. That's a lesson in life.

If I had beaten George Foreman that night in Las Vegas it would have changed my life significantly. George went on to become a major celebrity and write several books. Not to mention the George Foreman Lean Mean Cooking Grill which made him more money than he ever made in boxing.

The winner that night would never have to box again. The financial rewards for the victor were tremendous. It is the same in your life. If you had signed and closed that contract or got that promotion at work, it would have changed your life. Moments like that don't come around very often. Conduct your due diligence on your opposition. You must be prepared for whatever they throw at you. Always play to win.

Build Your Boxing and Business Skills

Much like a professional boxer or a business owner, your skills are developed over time. One month turns into one year and two years turns into five years. It is an acquired skill learning how to successfully manage a business or become an electrical contractor or a professional boxer. You just don't acquire these skills overnight. Much like boxing skills, your professional attributes can take years to develop and master.

> *"Be the student, be the teacher, and become the master. If you can transcend through these stages of life then you will conquer all."*
>
> *—Michael Moorer*

It's nice to write a book, do you know why? You can create your own quotes and publish them in the book.

What Are Some Basic Business and or Boxer Skills?

This list is going to sound like a business meeting.

1. Passion for what you do.

If you don't love what you are doing, there will never be passion in your life or work. If you don't love it, leave it.

2. Life is 85% mental and 15 % physical.

It's more inspiration than perspiration.

3. You must sacrifice to succeed.

What ever your profession; singer, dancer, football, boxing or business, you will have to sacrifice to be successful.

4. Change your life style.

To get to the top of business or boxing, your life style will have to dramatically change. It will be extremely difficult in the beginning but your life will get better.

5. Demanding and strict schedule.

You will and must become self disciplined. Learn to say "No." You are going to be busy. If you don't make it happen, who is?

6. Focused with a strong body and mind

Only the best in business survive. You only survive and excel with a strong mind and a strong body that follows. You can't have one without the other.

7. Driven – 10 year business plan to get to the top

Drive is passion and motivation combined. Be driven. Set goals and work to accomplish them. You will set one day, one week, one month goals, one year goals, five year and then ten year goals.

8. Demanding Work Ethic

Do you think you can gain fame and fortune and not work hard? If you actually believe that you can succeed without dedication and hard work, then put this book down and go to the pool.

It's funny. Two different kinds of people will read this book. First, those people who already have money and want more and secondly, the person who is economically struggling and wants a better life. Both are looking to increase their standard of living.

9. Be able to turn it on and turn it off.

It does not matter if you are a professional actor, boxing champion, teacher, construction foreman or a police officer; you have to know when to turn it on and when to turn it off. Learn this skill and you will become a leader. I'm talking about your demeanor, energy, attitude, and command presence.

10. Able to adapt to change

When a monstrous hurricane travels through the Southeastern United States there is massive destruction.

The 100 year old thick oak trees are broken in half and buildings are destroyed. But some trees and buildings are still standing, why? Because they are flexible and can adapt to changes.

The palm trees bend in the wind but do not snap or break. The old buildings sway with the wind and do not fall. As a leader or business professional you must learn to bend without breaking. You will have to learn to adapt to your surroundings, new bosses, or your opponent. That could be a change in your corporate management, the economy or a divorce. Learn to adapt and be flexible. Make the best of any situation. If you don't adapt you will be broken.

You too can adapt to change. How, try to relax, be flexible, think, listen, make small changes, and in the end you will prevail.

The dream of one day owning a fortune 500 company having your own restaurant is within your power if you want it. All you have to do is change from what you are to what you want to be. This change will not be easy and could take years.

NFL vs. CEO

We can all agree that to make it to the top takes, talent, dedication, perseverance, hard work and more. But once we get to the top what happens next. Most of us stop learning.

Imagine if you are an elite National Football League quarterback (NFL). You have made it to the big league. In college you were the Heisman Trophy winner and the nation's best college quarterback. In the NFL draft you were selected number one. You were the best of the best. You moved into your new team's headquarters and said to yourself, "I have finally made it."

So why train anymore. You are making 4 million dollars a year, got that new car you always wanted, bought a house and have a new contract. You say to yourself, "I'm set so why train for the season. I'll just wing it." That is exactly what hundreds of CEO's do every year and some of the new NFL draftees.

After years of hard work CEO's finally reach the pinnacle of their career and have been promoted to the Chief Executive Officer of the company where they have worked for the past 20 years. In their mind they have made it to the top and do not need any additional training. That is a mistake many executives make.

An analogy would be the NFL quarterback. How long would he last in the league if he never trained for another game? Never lifted weights, quit running and failed to attend the team meetings. He would be out of a job in two weeks.

Here is my point. You can never stop learning. Everything changes. If you own a corporation, every member of the company should receive training from the top to the bottom. Every day in the business world the market is constantly changing. New computers, shipping, invoicing, marketing strategies, or the price of cheese just went up. That's important if you have a pizzeria. Without regular training for all your personnel, you company will never get to the top.

Punches Thrown and Punches Landed

When you do something, do it with power. Make it count. Don't waste your time and energy making a watered down presentation to a possibly new client. Every punch, every meeting has got to be 100% maximum effort.

Let's look at the punch count in a boxing match. The boxer from Puerto Rico has thrown 300 punches and landed only 100 punches. Now, the other boxer from Mexico has thrown 250 punches and landed

125 punches. Who do you think is winning the fight? Most likely it is the boxer from Mexico who landed 50% or 125 of his punches. But, what if he just threw one punch that knocked out his opponent. Isn't that one punch better than all of the others?

It is the same philosophy in business. Be decisive. Make an impact on new clients and customers. Put some power behind projects that are assigned to you. If you get leads for new business and you make a faint hearted attempt to contact them, don't waste your time. But, if you take each lead and put some effort and power behind it and actually try to qualifying the lead, now you have put some muscle behind it and you just might close that deal and sell that person. That works. That's a punch that will count rather than just punching in the air.

An example would be, if you want to be an actor, then become that actor. Take acting classes and work hard to perfect your talent and craft. You have to showcase your talent. Keep trying, show up for auditions and keep yourself active. An analogy would be a punch thrown with power but the other boxer deflects most of it but it still lands with some power. If I keep hitting him with that same punch for four or five rounds, he is going to take notice. After awhile I will get through and the punch will count. He will know I'm there.

If you are an actor, keep acting. If you want to date the counter girl at your local restaurant, keep trying. If you diet, then diet and don't cheat. If you lose those 20 pounds, you will be amazed at the results. Keep trying until someone takes notice.

> *"Whether you think you can or you think you can't, you're right."*
>
> *—Henry Ford*

It all comes down to you. Do you want to do it and do you think you can? You have to have the desire to change before you even try. Positive thinking and say to yourself, "Yes, I can do this!"

Key Points of Round 4: Building your skills

- Education and training
- Determination and skill
- Focus on your goals
- Be ready when preparation meets opportunity
- Expect success
- Don't give up

Progressive Action Steps (PAS)   Completed

1. Team up with a teacher to teach you   ☐

2. List your goals   ☐

3. Practice your new skills   ☐

4. Join a sports related team   ☐

5. Changed one bad habit for a good one   ☐

6. Diversify   ☐

Notes

ROUND 5
The Quality of
Your Product or Service

"Quality is not an act, it is a habit."

—Aristotle

I'm not Perfect

In my lifetime I have made some good decisions and some bad decisions. Regardless of the outcome, I have always and always will take responsibility for my actions. Why should you or I be held accountable for our actions? The answer is that we had a choice and made the decision, good or bad. So we all have difficult times in our lives. The real measure of a person is how you handle adversary and what you do about it!

One thing I did do right was my climb to the heavyweight championship. I had a perfect record of 35 wins and no loses when I fought Evander. I had hired the right trainers, the best managers and my boxing skills were peaking at the perfect time in my career.

We took the Evander Holyfield fight at a risk. He was the Heavyweight Champ and was coming off a big win. He too was at the right time in his life to retain the championship belt. That was my night and not his. After the win over Evander I fought George Foreman ten months later and got knocked out. I was told I had won every round up to getting knocked out.

Whatever mistakes you have made in the past, get over it. It is time to quit beating yourself up over something you did years ago. Yes I know it may be traumatic or emotional. I understand that. We cannot change what has happened years ago. Learn from it. Visually close the door and try to forget about it.

Can you change what you did five years ago? The answer is a big fat "No." It is time for you to move forward and become that better person and don't make that mistake again. Start fresh again. Get rid of that mental and or physical baggage. Its history and don't go back there anymore. You and your body will rejuvenate once your new passion and drive kicks in. Look toward the future.

If you keep revisiting what you did wrong in your life you will never have the opportunity to do things right. You can't grow if you don't forget. Why don't we start today and focus on today and not yesterday?

Longevity in Your Profession or Business

To truly succeed in your chosen profession you have to have a quality product or service that people need. What sells today is a product or service that is new or different. This is what sustains a business through recessions or hard times. How good is your quality or service? Is your product sustainable? What you offer must be better than your competitor or you will have marginal results and no success.

In the business of boxing, what sells tickets? It is the showman ship of the boxer in the ring combined with his or her ability to knock someone out. This is what promoters and fans look for in a fighter. I look back on my career and I remember that I was not that friendly to the press. That may be why people see me in a restaurant and say, "You're that boxer…." They know the face but have forgotten my name.

It is important for you to use any tool you have that will get your name out there. It can be a product or service. Like they say, "Any publicity is good publicity."

Is your product or service a knockout? Does it have the "Wow factor?" What do people say about your business? Every time someone uses or purchases your product does the consumer say, "Wow, what a great product?" Does your service or product have its own name brand? Every boxer does. I was Double "M", Joe Frazier was "Smokin" Joe Frazier, and Cassius Clay was Muhammad Ali. Your name brand is important for product recognition.

What separates you from the competition? Did you ever have a warm Krispy Krème donut and a cup of coffee? Now that's what I'm talking about. That was a memorable experience. You product should be memorable. Do something different from the pack and stand out in the crowd.

You cannot be one-dimensional and expect to be there the following year. To have continued success you must have a great product. Times change and so do products. You have to adapt to the change and still continue to deliver quality.

NFL Great Jerry Rice

One good example of quality in action is the Pro Football Hall of Fame member Jerry Rice. He played for the San Francisco 49ers most of his career. He is without a doubt the greatest wide receiver to ever play the game of football. Why was he such a great football player? It was his preparation for every season and every game.

Jerry Rice was the consummate professional that kept getting better every year. His wife said, "We never went on vacation because Jerry would always be training." He was always striving to do what? The answer is "Get better," Your business has to get better every year and never have a bad game. That is what longevity is all about.

If you stay in business long enough or you are training for a professional fight, there are no vacations until you are at the top. That's right. You will work ten-hour days and take no vacations for years. You may not go on vacation for four or five years. Every day you work a little harder, a little extra, to give yourself the opportunity and a chance for success.

Higher Standard

It doesn't matter if you already have a business or you are about to start one. It is imperative that you hold yourself personally responsible to get to a higher standard. It could be a product, service, or you. Yes that's right, you. If you are an actor or paint houses for a living you must teach yourself to be the best damn actor or painter there is. You just can't be better than the other guy. You must excel at whatever you do. You have to constantly be improving your product and or your service. If you don't, your competition will.

> *"It's a funny thing about life; if you refuse to accept anything but the best, you very often get it."*
>
> —*W. Somerset Maugham*

Be the Best at What You Do

It doesn't matter what profession you choose during your lifetime. You may want to be a musician, plumber, doctor or a lawyer. But, whatever your choice of careers is I want you to strive to be the very best in that field.

How is this achieved? It is achieved by working hard, learning and staying focused. Remember, you may have passion but you still need to acquire the talent and or skills. Work hard and develop a good skill set.

Here is a quote from Randall "Tex" Cobb about being the best that you can be.

> *"Ernie Shavers could punch you in the neck and break both your ankles."*
>
> —*Randall "Tex" Cobb*

I don't want you to be the employee who does just enough to get by. No one really notices you and everyday is the same. This kind or type of person is going nowhere in life. If you are a waiter or waitress I want you to excel serving food and waiting on people. I need you to be the best waiter the restaurant has ever had. You have to excel at what you do!

It doesn't matter if you paint houses for a living, wait on tables or you are a professional boxer. Be at the top of the profession you choose. You are not going to love everything about what you do but you can still take pride in your job. You will be surprised at what happens if you take pride in your job, work a little harder and become the best. People will take notice.

George Foreman tells the story when he was growing up he washed dishes at a restaurant. If you ever washed dishes in a restaurant there is no lower position in the restaurant than the person who washes the dishes and takes out the garbage. George excelled at his profession of washing dishes. George took pride in his job. He was the best dish-washer the restaurant ever had. Do you think this positive attitude carried out to his boxing career? History can answer that.

> *"Men acquire a particular quality by constantly acting in a particular way."*
>
> *—Aristotle*

Your Health

You can never be the best at what you do unless you have good health. Better health means better wealth. Everybody has his or her own formula for being healthy. In the past twenty (20) years, you have seen the change in professional athletes. To be a star performer today requires the athlete to dedicate one-half of their time to the sport and the other half to being physically fit. The sport hasn't changed but the athletes and training methods have.

The athletes of today are training smarter and more efficient. They are stronger, bigger and faster. The competition has elevated itself to where every year new world records are being broken on a regular basis. Why, because the athletes are training smarter not longer.

The non-athlete business man or woman works 8-10 hours a day and then goes home and has a few drinks, smokes his/her cigar and watches television. Where is the training at? Where is the business training or the physical training? How can you expect to compete with your business competitors with a lifestyle like that?

Now, your competitor leaves work, goes directly to the gym, and works out for 1½ hours. He/she then goes out to dinner has green tea, a veggie burger and a low fat desert for dinner. Your competitor leaves the restaurant and goes home and sits down and reads four chapters on Gorilla Marketing or a book on financial planning. Who is going to be the peak performer?

No longer can we leave work and meet at the bar. Okay, I can't believe I just said that. We can't drink ourselves silly and chase the opposite sex until late that night, drive home and dive into bed. Get up the next day, do it all over again and be efficient at work.

What if I did train 8 hours a day? But after leaving the gym I drink beer and smoke cigarettes until midnight, forget to take my vitamins and then have dinner. I eat at the bar and have a healthy cheeseburger, French fries and coke. After a night out, I get home around 2:00 am, sleep until 7:30 am and then go to work. Am I going to be the corporate athlete that beats the competition? What do you think?

Your body is your only vehicle for making money. It is imperative that you take care of yourself. Take care of your body. If it doesn't work, you can't make money. Stay healthy. We know that you are going to start one day, how about today.

Your body is much like the engine in your car. Change the oil every 3000 miles, tune up every six months and use high test gas for better fuel efficiency. Eventually the miles will add up and you will need new engine parts. It's just part of life. Your body and the engine will grow old due to the miles you drive.

I just had my right knee completely replaced this week. It has been painful for years but I finally decided to get it done a few months ago. The miles I ran on concrete over the years took its toll now that I am 44 years old. Take care of yourself. If you need to replace the worn parts like I just did. If you don't feel good physically you simply cannot work at your peak performance.

The Pre-fight Boxing Weigh-in

As an athlete sometimes you have to lose body weight drastically to make weight for a fight. For example, many boxers weigh more between fights than the night of the fight. Part of the training regiment is to get down to their fighting weight.

The day before the fight, the weigh-in takes place. On most of my fights this was the first time I ever met or seen my opponent. Both fighters dress in shorts, no shoes or shirt and stand barefooted on the scales for an exact body weight. Usually my opponents will flex their biceps, growl at me or do something crazy like that. I thought it was funny when they did that.

A boxer may fight at different weight classes during his career. That is what I did. The older I got the more difficult it was to make weight at the lower weight divisions. I moved through the light heavyweight division without a loss and knocked out all of my opponents. Sports writers said that was a major achievement and historical in boxing history. When you win at multiple boxing divisions, you are considered a "multiple champion." Enough of my past career let's get back to the weigh in.

More takes place at the weigh-in than just getting the boxers weight. Since Muhammad Ali's weigh-in antics things have changed. The modern day weigh-in has become more of an event than just two boxers knowing how many pounds they weigh. It is now a photo opportunity for the press and also a chance for both boxers and their entourage to trash talk each other. I rarely trashed talked my opponent but I did go nose to nose with most of them to show I wasn't intimidated by their size or their boxing record.

What's funny is that as a heavyweight boxer we go through the ritual of being weighed in even though there is no weight limit to that boxing division. I could weigh 205 lbs. or 325 lbs. it doesn't matter. Just for the record, though the heavyweight category is 201 lbs. or more. Just below that is the cruiserweight category, which is 175 lbs.

Quick Weight Loss

My point in the previous paragraphs is that often I had to lose weight fast when I fought the lighter weight classes. This program works quite well as long as you take your vitamins and don't stay on it too long. Remember carbs are a form of fuel. You can get your good carbohydrates from other foods. This program lowers your carbohydrate intake and you lose weight fast.

White Out

This weight loss program works if you don't eat anything that is white. You will be drastically cutting out most of the complex carbohydrates that turn to sugar and fat in your body. On this short-term diet (2 to 4 weeks), do not eat any food substances that are white. Here is a short list of what <u>not</u> to eat.

- White flour
- Salt
- Sugar substitutes
- White sugar
- White rice
- White bread
- Milk or milk products
- Spaghetti/pasta (white in color)
- Potatoes
- Cereal
- Crackers

The "White Out" diet will cut your weight after the first week. You will see and feel the results. The simple diet is, if it is white, don't eat it. Try to eat green vegetables, chicken and drink a lot of water. I recommend this diet. It really works. I used it for several fights to cut weight fast. Give it a shot. You may like it.

Vitamins

In business or when life challenges you, an edge always helps. As a professional boxer we are all looking for that magical pill that will put us over the top. Sometimes that pill is vitamins and other forms of nutrition.

The science of nutrition has changed since my championship years. On the Olympic level, what the athletes eat is almost as important as their training schedule. You have to have the right fuel for different engines. Nutritionists are doing extensive studies to determine what athletes need for each sport.

If you are a farmer, doctor, actor, or a construction worker and you are trying to be successful in your chosen vocation, you need all the advantages you can get. I can guarantee that you are not eating right if you work your day job, come home and work on your home business or your 2nd job until 12:30 AM every night.

I am a big believer in vitamins and nutrition. I had a full time nutritionist during my championship run. Not everyone can afford the staff I had when I was the champion. Nevertheless, you can afford to take a multivitamin daily and a selection of other vitamins you may need. This is only a small part of keeping your body that fine tuned and oiled business machine.

Being healthy ensures your ability to work and perform at a higher level. Vitamins and nutrition combined with a physical fitness program could be the edge you need for your personal success.

Try this for one week. Walk 20 minutes, 10 sit ups and 10 pushups and take the multivitamin for the 7 days. The next week I want you to walk 21 minutes and do 12 sit ups and 12 pushups. You get the concept. Start slow with what you can do and build from there.

Give the Customer More Than They Paid For

In business, the quality of the product will stand by itself and then comes service. If you always give your customer more than what they paid, for you will always be assured success.

When I fought, to me it was "Show time." I was going to work just as you would be selling cars, working construction or working at the ER as a nurse. I did my best each and every time I fought. That's all your boss is asking from you at work, "Be the best you can be." Give your boss or your customer more than what they paid for. You will be surprised at the dividends this pays after only a short time.

Assertiveness

Before I close this round out I would like to talk about being assertive. Do not be afraid to be assertive. Lack of being assertive makes people or employees believe that you are weak. They will believe that you don't have what it takes to be successful. Is this the kind of image you want to project?

If I go into the ring and let the other person pound on me, who is going to win? I'm the champ. People expect me to do what…...win. If I don't go out there and show I'm in control, what happens? The other boxer takes over and will win the fight. Learn how to exercise control. It's like my left hand. I use it when I have to get the other boxers attention.

It is the same philosophy with employees. They want to tell management what to do. You can't have the tail wagging the dog. Learn to be assertive when it is necessary. You are in business to make money and not to have everyone like you. If you want someone or something to love you then go out and buy a puppy. People will respect you more for being assertive than being afraid to confront a problem when you are in the right.

Marketing Your Product or Skills

Where you market your products is just as important as the product itself. You will never see me in a boxing ring fighting with an advertisement tattooed or stenciled on my back.

Some boxers are getting companies to pay them to advertise their product on their back. I never did that and I think it is the wrong place to advertise your business. Especially if he gets knocked out in the first round. How are you going to read the advertisement when your live boxing billboard is on his back out cold and unconscious?

If your product is top notch, it will sell itself. If you repair shoes for a living and do a great job, your customers will refer you to their friends. The service and your leather skills will sell themselves. Could you imagine repairing shoes and just doing an "OK" job? Like they say, your best advertisement is word of mouth.

Never Stop Learning

If your skill is teaching, dancing or a being a waiter in a restaurant, it doesn't matter. You can always learn to be a better worker or individual. As a professional boxer, I never stopped learning. There are improvements on equipment, nutrition, training methods, stretching and the skills of boxing.

Did you ever watch Mike Tyson jab, jab, and then throw the uppercut punch? It was powerful and a thing of beauty. I watched him knock out a lot of boxers with that combination. In fact, I practiced it and used it once or twice in some of my pro fights. No matter what your skill, you can always learn more.

Set High Standards

Always set a higher standard for yourself. I didn't start boxing to be one of the top 3 or 4 boxers in the world. If you are going to do it reach for the stars! To reach the stars you must set a higher standard for yourself and want to be the best.

Where do you want to be five years from now? I wanted to be the champion of the world and not just a good boxer. Do you want to be an average writer, waiter, shift supervisor or just a good pianist? No! Get to the top. You become the best by not settling for mediocrity and working harder than the other person. The battle for perfection is in you and not the person you are competing against.

Remember your body changes and your skills change over time. You can learn something new every day. The key is to be at the top of your profession. Set the bar higher for yourself.

"We make a living by what we get. We make a life by what we give."

—Winston Churchill

Product Longevity

As a boxer my earning capacity is limited to just a few years. I get older and the competition gets younger and faster. It's just the facts of life. Times change and you change. Let's look at another example of a quality product, passion for what they do and still making tons of money. How about music, rock music?

Let us look at rock bands. The Ringo Starr's, the Rolling Stones, Aerosmith, Bon Jovi and the list goes on and on. You have three things here that work:

- The musicians love what they do.
- The product or music is still entertaining.
- Product longevity.
- They still put on an incredible show.

This is where you want to be. Number one, they don't need the money. They are all worth in the hundreds of millions of dollars. Secondly, they still have the passion to go to work and perform, why because they love what they do. Lastly, they never put on a bad show. The product they produce is still good and selling.

What you don't see is…think about it…new material or new songs. When was the last time the Rolling Stones had a hit or Paul McCartney was number one on the music charts? It doesn't happen. Ask yourself why? Is their creativity gone or are they just not as hungry as they were when they first started? The answer is maybe a little of both.

What does that mean to you? Let's say you own a restaurant. You love what you do and have never served a bad meal. If you can do this and keep doing it, you will be in business for a long time. If you are an actor, love what you do and never have a bad performance. If you make a product, love what you made and keep making your product better. This is what keeps us going. The absolute love of what we do.

Passion + Skill + Work Ethic = Success

Passion and Skill Creates Success

The qualities that make up a musician or a doctor are similar. These same qualities can be found in your best actors, Tom Cruise, Robert DeNiro and Jack Nicholson. What is that internal quality? They have passion for their profession.

All of these actors struggled in the beginning of their careers just as you may be now. Some were bar tenders, cooks, or worked as a plumber. The secret is that they never quit and still have great passion for the movie roles they play. When these professional actors work, they become the person they are portraying.

When Sylvester Stallone wrote the movie, "Rocky" in 1976, he was offered a small fortune for the movie rights and screenplay. Sly said, "No thank you. I'm going to star in the movie myself and have it produced." The big names in Hollywood laughed at this guy….Sly. Stallone who is this new guy on the block? He never wavered and the rest is history. The "Rocky" movies have grossed over 1 billion dollars.

The road you chose for your life is an internal conviction. The great ones have all felt it. Somehow, they believe they are "special" in some way. Ask Barbara Walters or Arnold Schwarzenegger. They all have that internal feeling of greatness. They can't explain it but all of them have that feeling they are destined for more in life than just mediocrity. Do you have that feeling that you should be better than you are?

74

Make a plan to get to the top and follow it. Be the best you can be. If you follow your passion and have the skills you need to be successful, nobody can stop you. It's up to you to go out and do it.

> *"Do or do not. There is no try."*
>
> *—Yoda*

If you just "try" in life you are never going to make it. People who say, "Well, I guess I will try it" never make it happen. You have to be inspired to do it. If you lack the motivation and desire then do something else. Like Yoda says, Do it or don't do it. But don't waste your time trying."

Key Points of Round 5:   Quality of Service or Product

- Plan on Longevity
- You can be the best
- Raise your standards
- Get Healthy
- Do you have the passion?
- Do you believe that you are "special"
- Be inspired to produce a good product

Progressive Action Steps (PAS)   Completed

1. Is your product top notch? ☐

2. Are you getting healthy? ☐

3. Do you give the customer more for than what they paid for? ☐

4. I have started to lose that weight. ☐

5. I purchased a multi-vitamin today. ☐

6. I am just going to do it for now on, no excuses. ☐

Notes

ROUND 6
Building a Team

"The way a team plays as a whole determines its success. You may have the greatest bunch of individual stars in the world, but if they don't play together, the club won't be worth a dime."

—*Babe Ruth*

It's Lonely at the Top

Personally, I don't mind being alone, sometimes. You will find that when you are at the top people treat you differently. When I was the champ doors opened easily for me. Everywhere I went I was treated like a king. The minute I lost the crown those doors were still there but I had to open them. Boxing is a one man show only in the ring. It took a team to get me there.

I can honestly say that during my best years in boxing most of my managers and training team were afraid of me. That is not good. You need your team to take you to the next level. They should not be afraid to tell you what you don't want to hear. I believed I knew what I needed to succeed but I was wrong.

Your success will be determined by the team around you. If you do not build a cohesive team, you will not be successful. You have seen this in team sports. One team owner goes all out and spends millions of dollars getting the best players together on one team. And, what happens? The team never jells into a single entity. You may have the best talent but the team was not cohesive.

Winning teams are built through leadership. Your team members must have the confidence in each other and the management or leader to get the job done. Remember the key to success is that all members work as a team and not as individuals.

You can be a one-man band and play at birthday parties or you can lead an orchestra that performs at the White House for the President of the United States. Which act do you want to be? You can't do it alone. Your time is limited, your skill set is limited and you are just one person.

Many businesses are family owned and operated. How many companies succeed when the entire family works toward one common goal? Create a family atmosphere in your team or organization. You will discover that you are stronger together. A team will always out perform a group of individuals every time.

Hire a Leader

The very first thing I ever learned about management or leadership, is someone has to be in charge or responsible. Assign that person the leadership position and make them accountable.

That happened to me in preparation for one of my fights. We went to camp in Pennsylvania where I could concentrate on nothing but the fight. When we got there and began to set up the camp, I found that no one....no one brought the equipment bag that contained the heavy bag gloves, tape, or hand wrap. I looked at my trainer and said, "Who was responsible to bring that equipment? He looked at the manager and said, "I thought you brought that equipment." He just shrugged his shoulders like, "I don't know." Leaders must delegate responsibility even down to the simplest level but they have to follow up to make sure the task is completed.

If you hire a strong leader to work with you there is something you have to understand. Let that person lead. That delegation of responsibility sometimes takes time for you to let go. You will get a lot more done if you learn to delegate.

That may have been my problem with my former trainers. I hired Steward, Georgie Benten, Lou Duva and Teddy Atlas to manage my career and train me. I look back and those were my best years as a boxer. There was just one little problem. I hired them to train me but I still wanted to be in control. I thought I knew what was best for me. I wanted to be in charge but they were telling me what to eat, how to eat, when to eat, how much to eat and where to eat. Some people need that but I thought I didn't.

My point here is if you hire someone to teach you a profession, let them lead and learn from them. It will be a difficult transition but remember you hired them because they have skills you don't possess. I was winning in boxing but I found out I needed a lot more skills than I had to get to the next level and fight the top ranked boxers.

There is the story and here is the teaching point. Hire someone that possesses the skills you do not have. If you had the nutritional, cooking, political or accounting skills they had, you wouldn't need them. Let them lead you.

Teams Are Built Through a Common Goal

The key to success is that all members of the organization work as a team and not as individuals. Men and women will follow a leader that has a visionary goal. They want to share that vision with the leader. That is what makes a team come together. Individuals become a team, when everyone has the same common goal.

As a boxer, everyone in my camp wanted to be part of a world championship team. Everyone had the same common goal and that was to get Michael Moorer to the big show. That big show was fighting for the title. In life, teamwork will take you a lot further than doing it by yourself. The important point of teamwork is that everyone on the team has the same common goal.

When you have a cohesive team, everyone is marching to the same beat. When the team is marching or working and someone is out of step that one person makes the whole team look bad. The team leader has to ask himself or herself, is that person marching to a different drum beat?

Here comes the tough part. If they are not part of the team then ask them to join the team and if they don't share the same team goals, then take them off the team.

If you ever play a sport or watch the super bowl on television, you can learn a lot about teamwork. Teams win championships, not a group of individuals. You will find that football teams, with the best team. wins game and not necessarily the best players. It is the chemistry or synergy of them all work together is what makes them winners.

Look at the Super Bowl XVII game on February 7, 2010, between the New Orleans Saints and the Indianapolis Colts. The Colts with Peyton Manning as the quarterback were heavily favored to win the game. The Indianapolis Colts were going to walk over the Saints. The New Orleans Saints ended up beating the Colts by the score of 31-17. The Colts had the best individual player talent but the Saints won the super bowl because they were the better team that day. Teamwork always outperforms individual effort.

Even though boxing is an individual sport, I needed a team to get me over the top. You can win for a while by yourself but soon you find you can't do it all alone. You will find that you need that support to achieve and set higher goals. Why, because a team will make you work harder and push you to the next level. You will ultimately discover that as a team, your performance levels increase and you will make a better decision than as an individual.

That is the strategy of the United States military. Recruits spend months and years with the same soldiers. They form a bond with each other. When they go to war, they go to war not as an individual soldier but part of a fighting unit. That's why when someone gets injured all they want to do is get better so they can re-join their unit in the field. Teamwork works.

> *"It's easy to get good players. Getting them to play together, that's the hard part."*
>
> *—Casey Stengel*

Surviving in Alaska

Here is one more example of teamwork. It is a classical case study used in many colleges for the masters program. The workshop is called "Surviving in Alaska." We did this in college where the end results showed us clearly that a team makes a better decision than one person. Using teamwork the decision was much better than that of a single individual. This is the scenario:

You are flying in the Alaska tundra and your plane goes down. Luckily you have survived the crash. You have crashed landed in Northern Alaska and have to walk out. You can only select and carry 10 items from the wrecked aircraft. You have to make a decision and decide what is important to take with you for your survival.

You also have to decide the items in order of importance. For example, is the knife more important than a thermo of hot coffee? Everybody in class picks the 10 items by themselves. Some of the choices of equipment are matches, snowshoes, gasoline, gloves, maps, compass, mirror, fishing line with hook, knife, ax, sun screen, water, etc.

The teacher has the list of items that were compiled by wilderness experts who survive in the arctic cold. The items or equipment is listed in order of importance for survival. She has the correct answers to the 10 survival items and the order of importance. Each student has listed, what they think are the most important survival items and in order. The teacher collects the individual student's top 10 survival items that have been written down by the student. Now she tells the class to get into groups of five students and do it all over again as a team.

You can hear some of the team members arguing that snowshoes are more important than gasoline and a compass is not as important as an ax. After approximately twenty (20) minutes, the teacher has the groups separate and asks for spokes person from each group to explain their list of equipment in order of importance.

The results from individuals are compared to the survival experts. For every one right you get 10 points and for everyone wrong you lose 10 points. The score of 100 is a perfect score. The teacher lists the scores on the board. Most of the individual scores are not bad usually in the 70's and some have 80 as a top score.

Now the teacher compares the top 10 survival items selected by the team that consisted of 5 students. This was compared to the individual scores or decisions. Each time the groups of five students scored higher than individual scores. The average group scores were 90% to 100% while the individual scores were in the 70's and 80's. This was a clear example where teamwork out performs individual decisions.

Tough Association

What a leader or a corporation doesn't need is "Yes Men." The "Yes man" tells the leader what he wants to hear and not what is important. He always wants to give the President good news but not what is reality. This type of individual destroys companies and team efforts. The team has to make the leader stronger, not by being soft but by telling the leader the hard facts and without candy coating the results.

How do I become a better boxer if all of my training partners let me beat them up? They would let me win every round while I was in training camp. People would be saying, "Boy the champ looks good tonight" but in reality my sparring partners are making me look good by not hitting me hard and letting me get through their defenses. I would be a paper tiger.

You make your team and leader stronger by working harder together. Everyone excels and gets better together.

Communication Is the Key to Team Building

You may be the CEO of your company or I may be the only guy boxing that night on HBO, but in reality you and your team are all working together. They are the vehicle that got you there. You build teamwork through good communications.

Hold meetings to get everyone on the same page. If you read the book called, "The One Minute Manager" the author recommends that you can hold one-minute meetings. In between rounds during a fight I have one minute to communicate with my trainer and my team.

During a boxing match, I have one minute between rounds to sit down, rest and get advice. Hopefully I can find the stool and go to the right corner. When I sit down, I meet with my trainer and cut man. They tell me exactly what I'm doing right and what I'm doing wrong. I have only one minute to catch my breath and get advice from my corner.

During one of my championship fights my trainer said, "Hit him with body shots this entire round." Body shots are a long term goal but they take their toll later during the fight. I heard what he said and the next few rounds; all I did was hit him with shots to his ribs, kidneys and lower abdomen. When I hit him in kidneys I buried my fist and glove as deep as I could into his body.

After several rounds, the boxer starts to feel the pounding on his ribs, organs and muscles. After a while, the organs start to suffer from the constant pounding. We had a plan for the future that worked that night. I knocked him out five rounds later and retained the light heavyweight championship. I could not have won that night without my corners help. During the fight they saw opportunities that I didn't see.

Building a solid team is important when you get together and plan strategies. You can't do it alone. Establish meetings with short term and long-term goals. Be open to suggestions. If you are at the top of your company or I'm in the ring, the team has a much better view of what's going on around you and they can give you candid advice. Make your meetings work. Hold people accountable in solving problems and planning for the future?

What plans or short-term goals does your company have? If you do establish goals, the most important part is the completion date. What date is the goal designated for completion? Without a completion date the goal is just a dream that has no deadline.

One final thought on communications is to get feedback from your team. Ask them for their input and advice. If you listen to what they have to say, the team will feel more involved in the overall success of the organization. Remember this motivational quote, "None of us is as smart as all of us."

Secret to Making Money

You want to know the secret to making money? You can fight George Foreman and make nine million or you can do it the easy way. Here it is. You make money but don't do the work yourself. Now you're asking me, Michael, how in the heck do I do that? It's simple; to make lots of money you have to duplicate yourself. This never happens in boxing but I have several friends of mine who have started small companies and made millions.

Let's look at a simple business plan that involves cleaning parking lots and taking care of the greenery. You know the owner of a local strip shopping mall. You start cleaning the parking lots and at the same time maintain their grass, bushes, trees and shrubbery. Most companies only offer the green maintenance or cleaning the parking lot. But you have combined both of them into one business.

You and a friend or family member invest in a parking lot sweeper, a lawn mower, and a few more tools. You guys are working from 10:00 PM at night until you finish the strip mall parking lot. It takes you about six hours to clean the parking lot and trim the shrubbery and trees. Both you guys are getting home around 4:00 AM after working all night. The hours are terrible but at least it's not hot and you are home before sun rise.

Other businesses take notice of how good the Denver Strip Mall looks and asks the owner who does the parking lot cleaning and the yard work. He tells him it's two (2) guys that sweep the parking lot and also cut the greenery. This strip mall owner now hires you to clean his parking lots and cut his grass. Now you have two malls and your working from 10:00 PM at night to 7:30 AM or 8:00 AM. You just doubled your business without paying out a dime.

After about a month, both strip malls are looking great. Every night they are cleaned and trimmed. Now you get a call from another mall owner who wants the same deal.

You and your partner split the shifts and you hire a third and fourth person to help with the new mall. Now there are four workers and three malls. Soon you get that fourth, fifth and sixth mall. You now have ten employees and you are doing more supervision than labor now. Now you assign a supervisor to each team and pay him just a few dollars more each night. You and your partner are now staying home at night while your teams are cleaning, sweeping, cutting and trimming. You have just duplicated yourself three fold. That's how you make money. You can now do something else but still maintain contact with the night crews until your supervisor is completely in charge. All you do is invoice and pay the workers. You get to keep what is left.

After ten months, you have gone from one strip mall to eleven. Your profit has gone from $1200 a month to over $10,000 a month. And the secret is you have reduced your hours from eight hours a night to eight hours a week.

Let's, quickly recap. What is the secret? The secret is to clone yourself. Find someone who has your experience and wants to work. That may be difficult but if you pay enough money, you will find the right people. Now let's talk about hiring someone to help you.

Secret to Hiring

Remember the saying, "Hire someone who will put you out of work." Learn to hire someone who is better than you. Pay them what they are worth. Your job now is to delegate the work and follow-up making sure the work is completed to your satisfaction. Sometimes it's just that easy.

Key Points of Round 6:   Build a Team

- Work hard
- Find the right people for your team
- Hire a leader
- Is your team cohesive?
- Does your team work well together?
- Duplicate yourself

Progressive Action Steps (PAS)   Completed

1. Have team meetings   ☐

2. Communicate with your team   ☐

3. Ask for feedback from your team   ☐

4. Practice the secret to making money   ☐

5. Delegate and follow-up   ☐

Notes

ROUND 7
Leadership

"The best executive is the one who has the sense enough to pick good men to do what he wants done, and the self-restraint to keep from meddling with them while they do it."

—Theodore Roosevelt 26th U.S. President

Success through Leadership

You don't have to be a leader to make money, start your own business or become a CEO, but it helps. What you will find is through the years in business you will assume the leadership role unintentionally and grow into the position. You will start making small decisions that eventually turn into big decisions. After a few years you are running the company and have assumed that leadership role.

Learning how to lead and leading people are two totally different things. Remember, leaders are not born they are developed. Most people are not leaders and want to follow someone. Whether it's your charisma, personal power or your ability to make money, you will attract a following.

Some people will follow you because you are charismatic or you can teach them something. Maybe you have that personal power they want in their lives. Others will follow you for their own personal reasons and some people just want to be part of your team, the winning team.

Are you a leader?

Many people do not want the responsibilities of being a leader. Leaders work harder and many times are held accountable for what occurs within the corporation or organization even though they are not the CEO. Being a leader is something internal. You want the responsibility and pressure and look forward to being accountable and responsible.

Leadership is a difficult task. If you really want to be successful and lead people, you have to able to govern yourself first by what principle, you lead by example. Nobody is going to follow you if you lack leadership qualities and especially if you can't produce winning results.

Here is a good example of leadership. Your football team is having a losing season, mostly because your quarterback has thrown more interceptions than touchdowns. One of the defensive team leaders calls a team meeting. You all meet in the locker room before the game. The quarterback stands up and starts talking and most of the team members throw their dirty laundry and towels at him and tell him to sit down.

Do you think the team is going to listen to anything the quarterback has to say? He is the reason why they are 3-11 on the season. He hasn't produced positive results; therefore he has absolutely no credibility with the team.

You will know you are a leader when accolades, trophies, compliments and kudos are not what motivates you. What drives you is the desire for results. Get that win, sign that company or getting that contract. This is exciting for you because ultimately it is good for your team, employees or organization. You have to produce being the leader.

You have to get something done that no one else can do. If you don't produce results, no one will follow you. They all want to be part of the winning team and not the losing team.

Purpose of Leadership

Leaders do not start out in life saying, "I want to be a leader." What you find out is leadership is a learned skill and not something you can buy. You earn the responsibility of leading people. Leadership is a trait that very few individuals have. Less than 5% of the general populous have the skills and want to lead.

Did you ever ask yourself why there are leaders? One reason is that you can get more accomplished leading people than doing it all yourself. In today's world, you have got to be a warrior leader. You must be an action-oriented person that first wants to be a leader and second has the ability to lead.

Most Important Quality of a Leader

Leaders are not born they are made. In the population today, less than 5% become leaders. That leaves the other 95% of the population to follow leaders. Which one are you?

After years of study and analyzing what makes a good leader, the results have shown that the single most important quality of a leader is Integrity. Integrity has proven itself to being the "X" factor in shaping and developing great leaders. Guess what? The single most important factor for success is, that's right you guessed it, integrity.

Not all leaders are successful and not all successful people are leaders. Remember what integrity is: It is what you do when no one is watching. Without integrity, there is no leadership. Albert Einstein said it well when he said, "Weakness of attitude becomes weakness of character."

"I don't know the key to success, but the key to failure is trying to please everybody."

—Bill Cosby

All Leaders Have a Vision

All good leaders have a vision. Coaches and politicians will say, "I have a vision for this team or I have a vision for this country." Some leaders see where they want to be in five years and take action to get there. They have a clear vision for the future. The great leaders are able to visualize their goals. If you are not sure where you are headed than how can you establish or set goals? Goals are the action steps you take to achieve a vision.

As a professional fighter, I had a vision. I saw myself as the heavyweight champ. It was as clear as day to me. My trainers and managers had goals but not the same vision that I had. What brings a team together is that everyone shares that same common goals or vision.

You can't have people on the team that are negative or hinder progress by not working. When I first started boxing, I wanted to fight anyone, anywhere. It didn't matter to me. I was young, motivated and had some boxing skills. On many of my fights my manager and trainer would say, "Michael you don't want to fight him. He has too much experience and you're not ready."

In my mind I had already fought my opponent, knocked him out and I'm looking for my next step up the boxing ladder. I fought them all anyway and beat every one of them. Don't let negative people hold you back. It's always good to get advice but listen to your instincts and never lose sight of your vision. More often than not, you are correct. You know your capabilities. All great companies and winning teams have a visionary leader at the top. That leader can be you.

The Dalai Lama says, "Share your knowledge. It's a way to achieve immortality."

Leadership Shared

It is important for a leader to share his goals and beliefs with other people. If they share the same values and objectives as the leader then a team begins to form. A good leader understands that his/her success is best achieved through leading a team.

Not everyone can be a leader but we all can be winners. Most people want to be lead. They want to follow winners and leaders and share their beliefs. They want to be part of the success that you achieve. Even though it is not theirs they still enjoy being part of the winning team and sharing it with you. They become winners through you.

Becoming a Leader

I attend many motivation seminars on peak performance and motivation. It gets me fired up and really motivates me. One thing all of the motivational speakers talk about is investing in yourself. What does that mean?

It is recommended that you take 10% of your income and use that money for yourself. One speaker I heard said that this is what made him the multi-millionaire he is today. With the 10% he joined the gym, purchased motivational tapes, bought vitamins, purchased nicer clothes, started buying a book a week, and started reading one hour a day. Why the reading?

If you read one hour a day, on the average you can read one book each week. That is 52 books in a year. To be well versed in a lot of subjects read 52 books on different topics that will intellectually stimulate you to seek out new challenges. You won't realize it but you will be smarter, feel good and are much healthier than ever being a success is almost guaranteed.

Now that you have improved yourself both physically and intellectually, your life will begin to change. The change will be slow but constant. Now you look like the leader that people want to follow. Now it's time for you to become the leader.

Winning Teams are built Through Leadership.

Be the leader of your company. Leaders are not born they are made. In the corporate business world it takes four years for a protégé to develop leadership skills. For four years, you work directly or underneath a proven leader. He or she becomes your mentor and you learn from the master.

It is the same parallel in boxing, martial arts or business. Take someone who has the raw skills and develop them by having them study with the master. This takes an average of four years but after a few years a leader is born. The education is costly but in the end, it will pay off in huge dividends. Like boxing or business, you have to practice to become a leader and a winner.

Leadership

The term leadership was first coined in the early 1400's. When the Nordic, English and Spanish Armada ships traveled across the Atlantic Ocean there was always one ship out front. The ship guiding or leading the other ships was called the Leadership. Thus the term "Leadership."

The Leadership would do the Following:

- The Captain with the most experience would be out front.
- The ship out front would lead so all of the other ships could follow.
- Make decisions that affect the fleet of ships.
- Guiding light at night, during storms or times of high risk.
- Out front and sets the pace.
- Sets the course, speed and direction of travel.
- Assume the risk of being out front.
- Guide the other ships.
- First ship to encounter risks.
- Leads the ships around storms.
- Take responsibility for their actions.
- Make critical decisions.
- First to engage and confront danger.

When Christopher Columbus crossed the Atlantic with three small ships the seas were uncharted and dangerous. Some still believed the world was flat and ships would fall off the earth if they went too far out to sea. But, in every Armada or group of ships one would be designated as the leader ship. The other ships would key off what that ship did. After many maritime years the term leadership began to evolve where it was not only used in nautical terms but also in management. Thus the word "Leadership."

Leadership Skills

- Integrity
- Motivates personnel
- Sets standards
- Action oriented
- Clear expectations to staff
- Instinctive
- Sets goals
- Self motivated

- Takes pride in your profession
- Commitment to the organization
- Commitment to your personnel
- Leads by example

The (3) Most Important Qualities of a Leader

What are the three most important qualities of a leader?
General Schwarzkopf had it right when he said:

1. Make the decision
2. Take responsibility for your actions
3. Always do the right thing

Good Leaders Inspire others to do Right

Leadership is something that grows on you. It is a skill that is acquired over time. Leadership is something you earn. It is not awarded. But good leaders do more than just lead. Great leaders inspire people to do the right thing.

What is the right thing to do? It could be join the team, get involved, work harder, and volunteer your time at a hospital. Sometimes leading even means putting your life at risk. In times of war soldiers followed their leader into battle without hesitation or question. Why, because it is was the right thing to do? They will follow their leader, anywhere.

5 Things a Leader Should do Every Day

1. Thank several employees for working for him/her
2. Smile and shake their hand.
3. Try to remember their names.
4. Ask them, "Is there anything I can do for you."
5. Keep a note pad in your pocket and write down their concerns or suggestions.

Leadership and Confidence

Over time I developed confidence in my right hand, remember I am a southpaw. After years of trial and error and working that jab, I became confident I could knock somebody out with one punch with my right hand or left hand. The same confidence applies to leadership.

You have to have confidence in yourself to be a leader. Good leaders know who they are. They also know their individual strengths and weaknesses. Confidence is a leadership trait or that all leaders possess.

Many times leaders are forced to make critical decisions when no one is available for advice. You have to have that confidence in yourself, the leader within you, to make those hard decisions. The worst action or non-action you can do as a leader is not make a decision. By not making that decision, you have fundamentally made one.

Our greatest responsibility as leaders is to make it happen. You have got to get the job done. You may be the president of a bank, a softball coach or the CEO of Coca Cola. It all falls on the leader's shoulders. We must be successful and have the confidence to make responsible decisions. When you have confidence, people recognize it. As a boxer, I was never cocky but I was confident. Many times that just scared my opponent to where he was beaten before I even entered the ring.

Make it Happen

Successful leaders just make it happen. They have the ability to make the right decisions. This is not a gift but a learned skill. The leader's success is made possible by supervising his or her staff and taking those individuals to that next level. They learn how to perform at a higher level by watching you. It is your job to empower them and teach them how to lead.

One of our greatest failures as a leader is not developing the potential in the people who put their trust and faith in you. It has been documented that it takes four years for someone to learn how to lead from a leader. It is our responsibility as leaders to make them perform at a higher level. Notice I didn't say teach, learn, help but make them perform. I think the work I am looking for is "delegate."

This is a regular occurrence in boxing. I will get a sparring partner before a fight and discover that this kid has talent. When we spar I can see his knowledge, skills and boxing abilities. These are called The KSA's term is quite often used in management. Even though he may be an opponent one day, it is my responsibility to teach him to be a better boxer today. It is our responsibility as leaders to teach and help everyone reach their personal potential.

Supervision

As a manager or business owner, you must never confuse activity for results. An activity should end with a result. Don't look at activity and think that it is a result, it is not. He looks busy but it's like the boxer who throws one-hundred punches a round but gets knocked out two rounds later. That's a result. You should measure success on accomplishments and not activities.

As a supervisor, we measure employees on results and not activities. When you are a supervisor, you have to see everything. Remember the word supervisor came from the word– super vision (eyesight).

First Impressions and the Pre-fight Stare Down

It doesn't matter if you are trying to pick up a beautiful woman in a bar, applying for your first job or at the weigh-ins at the world heavyweight boxing championships, first impressions matter.

Just before the fight the referee is giving instructions and what are the two boxers doing. Staring each other down. I'm not listening to a word the referee is saying. Did you ever wonder why boxers stare at each other, don't make eye contact and try to get as close as possible without touching their opponent….intimidation and fear. They want to see who will back down first. Then touching the gloves is another chapter.

You want to make a good first impression when he first sets his eyes on you. I want him to think I am one big nasty son of a bitch who has no fear and who is going to beat him into unconscious during the fight. It's all show. First impressions in business and professional boxing are important.

Mike Tyson was infamous for staring at his opponent when he entered the ring. Mike would look directly at his opponent and would not blink until the other person looked away. That is when Iron Mike

Tyson knew he had his opponent beat before he threw his first punch. It was Mike's form of psychological warfare.

When you apply for a job interview or you are trying to sell your product, first impressions set the tone for the meeting. When you first enter the interviewer's office and walk across the room and extend your hand the boss is looking at you and immediately forming all kinds of first impressions about you.

First impressions: What do they see first?

- Skin Color
- Gender
- Age
- Appearance
- Your posture
- Facial Expressions
- Eye contact
- Personal space
- Movement
- Touch-confident hand shake

Your interviewer is forming all kinds of first impressions as you walk across the room, shake hands and sit down. The moment you walk into the room he/she is evaluating you with his eyes. After you have introduced yourself and sat down, the interviewer probably heard very little of what you just said.

First impressions that last forever are made during the first two (2) minutes of any meeting and they are extremely hard to change. Ever heard the term, "Lasting first impressions."

It doesn't matter what you say the first two (2) minutes. The interviewer is still processing all of the above information. Did you know that?

- 55% of your meaning is conveyed non-verbally
- 38% is the sound and tone of your voice
- 7% is what you are saying

What does all this mean, when you first meet someone on a blind date, a business meeting, at the bank trying to get a loan or your opponent in a boxing match? In the first two minutes, it's not what you say it's what you sound like and look like.

If you are under dressed, wearing the wrong tie or sound insecure when you start your introduction, it's over. There is a good chance you have already lost the interviewer. You will not get that job you needed, or get a date with the woman you are talking to in the bar and I could lose this fight. That is how important first impressions are. You only have one chance to make a first impression, make it a good one.

Look and Act like a Leader

If you ever want to lead and be successful, you have to look the part. No one is going to follow you if you don't believe in yourself and secondly care about yourself. If you don't care about yourself, why should they follow you? In a jovial way one day at a press conference, someone asked me, "Hey champ, why have you and your girlfriend been together so long?" I answered, "Because we both love the same person….me." If you don't have respect or care about yourself how can you expect other people to respect and care about you?

Have you wondered why a military general or the President of a military power wears all of those medals and braids? The guy is wearing ten to twelve large medals and has gold braids on his shoulders. Anyone who can see all that brass and metal is in awe. You have to look the part.

That is why it is so important to look and act like a leader or a successful person. If I meet someone and I'm dressed in ragged clothes, what are they going to say to their friends? Yesterday I met Michael Moorer the heavyweight champion of the world and he looked like he needs a job. It all goes back to first impressions. What do they say, "dress for success?"

Now that you look the part, be the part. People expect certain things from leaders. They look for someone who can make a decision and someone who is not afraid to take risks. But most importantly makes the right decision by doing what is right.

Did you ever notice when you are with someone with authority that waiters, valet personnel and new acquaintances call them "Boss." They do not know the person but they can see the confidence and leadership ability by the way the person carries himself. That is personal power.

Boxing Fame

That is the caveat when you have some fame. Every person you meet will judge you from that very short period of time they spent with you. It could be five minutes, five hours or five days. I'm aloof, cold, arrogant or insensitive if I don't take that one minute and act like the champ and make that fan feel important.

I will always take a few minutes and shake a few hands, pose for a picture or two and sign some autographs. If I didn't take that few minutes each day, I will be labeled for life as being insensitive from those few boxing fans.

In your position, you might be the CEO or president of your company and meet some of your employees. Take a few minutes, talk to them, and ask them how they are. Be the leader that you are. Be the leader they expect you to be. That's why it is so important to dress the part and act like a leader and be the successful person you are.

> *"What you do in the boxing ring makes you famous. What you do outside the ring makes you infamous."*
>
> —*Michael Moorer*

In my boxing career I did have a few problems but nothing serious. You won't read my name in the newspaper headlines. I spend my off time with my children and show them I love them. I have always tried to lead by example.

The Keys to Success

There are two things I loved about Teddy Atlas, my former trainer and manager. First, he was a great ring tactician. He had the first three (3) rounds of the fight tactically choreographed. He knew the mental and tactical part of the boxing business.

Secondly, he was a terrific trainer and coach. He not only showed me how to box but also made me understand exactly what I was doing at any moment in the ring. He knew the in's and out's of being a trainer and how to motivate and train his fighters. The same principle applies to running a company, restaurant or a football team.

Failure to properly train yourself and employees is a huge reason why so many companies fail.

Philosophy of Training:

- Tell me ....I forget
- Show me.................I remember
- Make me do it............I understand
- Make me do it again.....I will remember, understand and will not forget

The above was taken from a Confucius quote where he says: "I hear and I forget. I see and I remember. I do and I understand."

The third quality of Teddy Atlas is that he was a great motivator. He knew what buttons to push to get a reaction from me. We all need a little motivation in our lives to jump start our career.

Someone Must Be Accountable

If you want to achieve success as a leader it is paramount that you delegate responsibility. Yes, that is right. You have give up some of your power. With that said, you should assign responsibility to a task but ultimately know that you are accountable for the outcome.

Once you have delegated the task, you can have only one person in charge and accountable for the actions of many. That person knows it is their responsibility to get the job done. You learn in business "shared responsibility is no responsibility." If you can't point to one person and say, "What happened" then there is no accountability.

"Men make history, and not the other way around. In periods where there is no leadership, society stands still. Progress occurs when courageous, skillful leaders seize the opportunity to change things for the better."

33rd President of the United States from 1945-1953

—Harry S. Truman

Key Points of Round 7:   Leadership

- Leadership is not an individual sport
- The number one quality of a leader is integrity
- All leaders have a vision
- First impressions are lasting impressions
- Look and act like a leader
- People will want to be associated with a true leader
- Leaders help other people get what they want

Progressive Action Steps (PAS)   Completed

1. Start learning how to lead   ☐

2. Start acting like a leader   ☐

3. Observe and model other leaders   ☐

4. Make decisions and be accountable   ☐

5. Create a team all with the same common vision   ☐

6. Spend 10% of your income on yourself   ☐

ROUND 8
Physical and Mental Toughness

"When there is fear of failure, there will be failure."

—General George Patton

Physical and Mental Toughness

An important characteristic of a champion is that they must be physically and mentally tough. Being physically tough means, you can take a beating and still continue to perform. Being mentally tough is when you are beaten physically but mentally you will yourself to continue to perform. The mind forces the body to keep going even under extreme conditions.

Against the Ropes

In life or boxing the worst place to be is against the ropes. You get pushed into a corner and just can't seem to get out. It doesn't matter if you are a boxer, a lawyer or a professional cook. You are doing the best you can but still you are getting the crap beat out of you. You're getting divorced, owe back taxes, fire burnt down your house and now you find out you are getting laid off due to the economy. How do you survive?

In 1974 in Kinshasa, Zaire, Muhammad Ali used the ropes to beat George Foreman. The fight was called, "The Rumble in the Jungle." George pounded Ali for eight rounds while "The Greatest" rested. In the final seconds of the eighth round, Muhammad Ali knocked out George

Foreman. The champ had expended all of his energy punching Ali against the ropes. When you are against the ropes, you are either resting or you are afraid, which is it?

We all have tough times in our lives when we feel as though the world is just pounding us into submission. It could be you lost your job, your wife just left you or that large account you needed chose another firm. You couldn't feel any worse about yourself or your life. Nothing works, you are tired and you hurt. You feel like giving up. Don't!

This is the time for you to get up off the canvas or off the ropes and fight your way out. Change your attitude from being defensive to now an offensive attacking mode. That is what Ali did to beat Foreman. Create solutions to solve your problems. If you do nothing but stand there and let the world keep pounding you, nothing will change. You will not be successful. So get off the ropes. You need to start moving and punching back. This will give you some room to breathe. Now face your problems head on and do something to get yourself out of the corner you are in. If you don't create movement and fight back, you will surely lose.

It is the same in life. Everyone has hard times but experience will tell you, it's not the hard times that's important but how you deal with the problem. If you want to survive, get off the ropes and get back in the fight. When your daily problems cannot look any worse that is the time you fight back and challenge yourself to become a winner.

Taking Care of You

Many successful businesses are owned and operated by a single person. That business could be a restaurant, an accounting firm or a mechanics garage. You have employees but you soon find out that you are the driving force behind the company. If you don't do it, it probably doesn't get done.

Managing your own company means long hours, a lousy diet, no exercise, and little time with your family or friends. Let's not even discuss taking a vacation. You are tied to your company and you are the glue that keeps it together.

When I was a professional boxer, I was the business and the product. In reality, you are the "business." I did everything I could to make sure the business remained successful. To have a successful boxing career my first priority was to take excellent care of myself. I focused on the development of my body, my mind, my spirit, and my daily regimen. I did this to keep the business of boxing going.

What would happen if I broke my hand, got cut sparring or had a serious injury and couldn't fight? I am the corporation and the product. Without me, without you, the money train stops here. The bottom line is that everything revolves around you as the central point of the business and that is not good.

What does my trainer and manager do? He trains someone to replace me. If I start getting beat and cannot make him money he has another boxer ready to step up into my boxing trunks. It's just business. As a businessperson, you should always train a trustworthy employee the skills to replace you. That way if you get sick and can't work the business machine keeps making you money.

Longevity Success

Protect yourself because you are an important and valuable asset to the company. If you are not there, your company has a problem. If Michael Moorer doesn't fight, I don't get a paycheck and neither do my trainers and sparring partners. To replace you in the company it would take five (5) employees. Isn't that right? You make things happen. It is important that you take good care of yourself so you can continue to perform at peak performance.

To have longevity and be effective in life you have to be physically and mentally fit. I can't go into a boxing match and not be at the top of my game. Remember, you are the breadwinner for your family. Pay attention to your lifestyle. Change it if it's slowing you down. Exercise, eat well, and get the required amount of sleep your body needs. The more fit you are, the better you will handle stress and are able to work longer hours with no days off.

Mindset of a Champion

True champions push past the pain and discipline to win championships. They do not let personal feelings interfere with their performance. The psychology of peak performance and mental toughness go hand in hand. Body, mind and spirit will get you through the tough times. The tougher you are mentally the more success you will have in life and love.

In our first fight, Evander Holyfield knocked me down in the second round of the Heavyweight Championship of the World, I thought, "damn that was a good right hand power punch." I wasn't hurt. I was mad that he knocked me down. . In fact, I was "fighting mad."

I knew then that this fight was going to go to the wire. It was either him or me. Who wanted to win more? I did and that is what happened. He was the champion and now it was my turn. I had to take it from him. Do you think Evander was just going to let me take it without a fight? I was hungry and had prepared myself mentally and physically to be tougher than my opponent. The fight went the full 12 rounds with me winning the majority decision. Whew, that was a close one. I was the new Heavy weight champion of the world.

> *Muhammad Ali once said, "When you can whip any man in the world, you will never know peace."*

Tough Business

Business or boxing is not for the faint hearted. Do you have any idea what it feels like when big George Foreman hits you in the face with a right hand? I've been hit so hard that sometimes I had no idea where I was, let alone in the fifth round of the heavyweight boxing championship of the world.

You are going to have days when you doubt yourself. Can I really beat Evander Holyfield? Is George Foreman too big and too strong? Should I fight Mike Tyson or stay away from him? Should I buy that product and put the success or failure of my company on the line? These are difficult decisions and they can change your future. My best advice is to do your homework. Listen to your instincts and make the right decision.

To start a business or becoming a professional boxer will take years of hard work and determination. You train and work out in dingy boxing gyms before your first fight. It will be thousands of hours before you

104

make your first paycheck. To become a world champion or a successful businessman or woman takes perseverance, dedication and long hours.

Winston Churchill said, "It's not good enough that we do our best, sometimes you have to do what is required."

Do you know anyone in business who is successful that doesn't put in long hours? Most successful small business professionals work Saturdays, Sundays and sometimes on Christmas. They are working while their friends are out having a good time. Plan on long days but if you put the time in, get something done. It's not how many hours you work each day but what you get accomplished during those hours. That is what really matters.

The Corporation

I am the Michael Moorer Boxing Corporation. Like most corporations, I am alive and breathing. You can feel it when your company is growing. Times are good; money is flowing in faster than you can spend it. Everything is running smooth. All engines are running at full throttle. You feel like a million dollars and the suddenly bam, you get hit, the economy takes a down fall.

You can feel your company hurting. That's what I felt like when I fought George Foreman. I was running on full throttle. I had won all of the first 10 rounds. Old George was on his last leg. But being the warrior that he is George reached down, dug deep and came out with two right hands. I saw the first combination but not the second. I was hurt and went down. That hurt. You have to expect and anticipate problems in your company. But like the right hand, sometimes they just come out of nowhere.

So, it doesn't matter if you are Michael Moorer or a corporation. We prosper, we fall down, companies sleep, we take hard blows, get knocked down and hopefully get right back up and get back in the mix.

As an executive of a company, you have to keep fighting and never give up. Your staff is looking at you for leadership and guidance. You have to protect yourself, your employees and the company. Think. React. Make good decisions. That's what good corporate presidents do.

Your Body Is Your Business.

Pretend that you drive a taxicab for a living. Your livelihood depends on that vehicle running mechanically sound and being able to drive 10-12 hours every day. The cab must have good tires, be tuned up, air conditioning working and in good shape overall. If the taxi cab is out of service due to a mechanical failure and is in the shop you don't make any money.

Now pretend your body is the taxicab. You work every day but do not take care of yourself. You are out late, eat bad food, drink every night and sleep 4-5 hours each day. Your system is running on empty. If you are not healthy or in the hospital, how can you perform at a high level? Bottom line, you can't.

Your health is the number one priority for change. You may have to lose weight, change your eating habits, take vitamins or begin to get back in shape. If you do this, you will have more energy and start to feel good about yourself. It's time to start taking care of yourself.

Here is the secret. Many doctors say that there are two things for great health. The first one is have a good breakfast in the morning. That fuels your body for a good workday.

The second secret to good physical health is to walk thirty (30) minutes each day without stopping. Get a good pair of sneakers and walk exactly fifteen (15) minutes in one direction away from your house or office. Why, because now you have to walk the fifteen (15) minutes back to your house. It's a no brainer and you can't fail. If you do this, you will live longer, be healthier, be more productive and look like a champion.

If you do not take care of your health, it's much like a mechanic not taking care of his tools. How long do you think you are going to be in business?

Be Tough

The tougher you get, the more success you will have. There are numerous varieties of toughness in this world. There is emotional, physical, and mental toughness just to name a few. But mental toughness has its own category. It stands alone. Toughness is one of the keys to greatness. In boxing or business, this is the inner strength that will lead you to success.

Boxing, like any business, is not for the faint hearted. Do you have any idea what it feels like when big George Foreman hits you in the face with a right hand? Bam, it rattled my entire body. After our last fight I had blood in my system for over a week. Boxing takes its toll physically and mentally.

Bam, bam, I hit George Foreman twice but he doesn't go down. Now it's his turn. I know it is coming but I can't stop it. I'm within his range and George starts pounding me with body shots and then one to the head. Whether you are a boxer or a businessman you take shots every day. It takes courage and mental toughness to be in either business.

I've been hit so hard sometimes I had no idea where I was. That happened once in the fifth round of the world heavyweight boxing championship fight with Evander Holyfield. Not a good time not to know where you are!

We all have days where we doubt ourselves and are unsure of our future. That's Ok because you will get past that. It's only natural. Your confidence will kick in and you will again focus on your objective. Have faith in yourself, have confidence in your abilities and the determination to see it thorough. You will be just fine.

It is risky opening a new business. The chances of starting a business today and it being successful are extremely low. Most businesses fail within the first two years.

Should I open a new business? Can I beat Lennox Lewis in England? Self-doubt left unchecked eats away at your mental toughness and ability to perform. Can I really beat Evander Holyfield? Is George Foreman too big and too strong? Should I fight Mike Tyson or stay away from him?

Making it through the business day or through another round of boxing is all about staying focused and remaining mentally tough. The battle is within you and it is both physical and mental.

Champions believe in themselves. Remember Muhammad Ali? There never was a more determined and confident boxer. He thought he could beat everybody and he did. He knocked down and beat the invincible Sonny Liston. Many experts thought Liston was going to be the champion for years until Ali fought him. In order to succeed you must first believe that you can. Ali had no doubt that night that he could beat Sonny Liston who Ali had nick-named "the bear." This is not the best English but believe that you can, and you can.

I met Muhammad Ali for the first time in August of 1994. I was in New York celebrating my win over Evander Holyfield. I went to an event and for the first time got to meet Mohammed Ali. He sees me and with his right hand motions me to come over. He puts out his right hand and we shake hands. As we are shaking hands he pulls me close to him for a man hug. He then whispers in my ear, "You're one bad nigga." We both laughed. It was a true honor to finally meet Ali "The Greatest."

Mental toughness carries successful people through stressful situations and times of uncertainty of self-doubt. Always believe that positive things happen to positive people. You can get through this, just hold on a minute longer.

"Courage is fear holding on one minute longer."

—General George Patton

Key Points of Round 8: Physical and Mental Toughness

- Longevity is important to your success
- Take care of yourself physically
- Get off the ropes and move forward in life
- Create a winning mindset

Progressive Action Steps (PAS)   Completed

1. Start walking 30 minutes each day   ☐
2. Eat a healthy breakfast   ☐
3. Start believing in yourself   ☐
4. You are what you think about   ☐

ROUND 9
Perserverance

"A man who never quits is never defeated.

—Richard M. Nixon- 37th US President (1969-1974)

World Heavyweight Championship Fight

When I fought Evander Holyfield for the first time it was in 1994 for the world heavyweight championship title. He knocked me down in the second round. I dropped my left hand and he caught me coming in with a good right hand. Bam, down I went. It was more of a flash knockdown than a punishing hit. But I still went down to the canvas.

When a boxer gets knocked down three things happen. One, your opponent becomes extremely confident and goes in for the kill immediately after the knockdown. Two, the ring judges automatically start scoring the boxer higher based on him knocking you down and three, I've got ten seconds to get up, breathe, clear my head, get through this round and most important try to win the fight.

I could have quit that night but I didn't. I came back and won the later rounds and beat Evander. The point is that you must never give up. If you want something bad enough, go get it. It could be love, a new car, keeping your corporation alive, becoming a rock star or a champion in boxing. If you quit, you will never know what it feels like to be a winner.

Sacrifice for Success

Becoming a professional boxer takes years of hard work and determination. You work out of a basement, a small gym or garage for the first three years and put in thousands of hours before you make your first paycheck.

To become a world champion in any sport or to be successful in any business takes perseverance and long hours. Success in your life will not come easy. You will work holidays, weekends and nights. When all your friends are out on dates, partying or on vacation, you will be hard at work trying to build your future.

When I first started boxing, I just didn't come off the street and fight Evander Holyfield or George Foreman. It took years to get to that moment in time when I was guaranteed the big paydays.

After 15 years of sacrifice and focusing on my goals, I was able to fight George Foreman. For that fight I was guaranteed 10 million dollars. To get to that point in my boxing career it took millions of dollars to prepare myself to be able to compete at that level. But, I did it. I fought George Foreman for the world title. I had the title and he wanted it. If I would have ducked rather than weaved at the moment he hit me with that straight right hand I probably would have won the fight. It was an extremely difficult loss after working so hard to get to that stage in my boxing career.

Do you know anyone who is successful in business that doesn't put in long hours? Most successful small business professionals work Saturdays and most Sundays. They are working while their friends are out having a good time. They work 10 – 12 hours a day and weekends. They have invested their life savings and time to make the business grow. You have to sacrifice a lot to be successful and accomplish your dream.

"**Everybody wants to go to heaven but nobody wants to die.**"

—*World Heavyweight Boxing Champ Joe Louis*

Success Takes Funding

Many new businesses will fail this year due to not be properly funded or undercapitalized. In your first three years in business, you will put thousands of dollars of your own money into the business. You will make mistakes that will cost you a lot of money. Also you have to have a nest egg to survive on your first three to five years in any profession that you choose.

Do you think I made a million dollars my first fight? No, in fact, my first paycheck as a boxer was when I fought Adrian Riggs. I grossed a whopping $400.00 from that fight. After expenses, I made $220.00.

It is the same parallel in boxing as business. You don't make millions of dollars your first year. In boxing you don't make "the big money" until you have over 25 wins and no loses. Many boxers don't even get to see any of the real money unless they are ranked in the top ten.

It is the same in business or the sports world. Professional football may be called a sport but believe me, it is all business. It's all about winning and not losing. If the coach doesn't win after a few years he is fired. The investment in that football team could feed several countries for a year.

You have to work hard for success and take each year to get better and improve your record. So when the time comes hopefully your corporation has prepared itself for that large contract or opportunity. You have to survive at least 2-3 years to give yourself a chance for success.

Sports and business are very much the same. A new corporation or a new football franchise will find it difficult to survive the first few years. New football franchises have great difficulty in having a winning record their first season of football. It will take great energy and a lot of money to achieve your potential and become a winner your first year.

The point is that in business or boxing you have to have capitalization and enough money to grow. It's a five or ten year plan. You are not going to make a profit immediately. Remember, I lived in a basement my first couple years as a pro. There is enough pressure as it is, to be successful, without having to worry about not being funded properly.

Here is the point. Don't be underfunded in your sport, corporation on dream. The problem with boxing or business is that there are no sure winners.

Passion for What You Do

There are three characteristics present in every successful boxer or business professional. The three "x" factors are:

1. Passion
2. Ability to work long hours
3. Become a peak performer

Passion

Never give up on your passion. Such great business minds as Walt Disney went bankrupt 13 times before he accomplished his dream of Disneyland and Disneyworld. He never got discouraged or lost his drive or passion to have his dream come true. Take a minute to imagine that he failed 13 times before he succeeded in creating the Disney parks.

Ability to Work Long Hours

Success will not and does not come easy. It will take years from your life and thousands of hours of your time, just to have a chance for success. That is where passion kicks in and takes you over the hump. This will give you a chance to succeed.

Prior to a fight I spent tens of thousands of dollars on training camp, nutritionists, chefs, sparring partners etc. there was no guarantee of winning my next fight. There is no guarantee you will win but that is what makes you work even harder for that one moment in time when you are the champion, get that part in the movie, or your child comes home from school with all "A's" and says, " I love you and thank you for being tough on me." That, my friend is success.

Business and boxing are not 9 to 5 jobs. As a professional boxer you are working 24/7. Sleeping a certain amount of hours, eating right, exercise, nutrition, video and film study, stretching, running etc. You eat and sleep getting your body and mind ready for a fight. There are no days off in running your own business or being a professional fighter. There is a direct ratio to how much time you put in and success. After a while, you get use to the regimented schedule.

A friend of mine coaches football at one of the top twenty ranked universities. He is an assistant coach for the offensive line. His day begins much like mine at 4:00 AM. I'm finished for the day around 3:00 PM while the coach is only about half way through his day. Sometimes he works so long he just sleeps in the player's locker room rather than make that drive home. When he gets home, he sleeps 4 hours and then drives back to the college campus. To be a champ you have to put the hours in.

"Do what you can, with what you have, where you are."

—*Theodore Roosevelt*

Peak Performance

In boxing, age limits your possibilities but not in business. Take for example Ray Kroc, the founder of McDonalds. His first restaurant was opened when he was 52 years old. You saw the yellow arches when you were growing up. The restaurant signs would say "1 million served." We all should have bought McDonald's stock.

Most of the conquistadores from Spain who traveled across the ocean were all in their 60's.   Age is not an excuse for success. Peak performance is a byproduct of passion and commitment.

When workers feel tired, are not motivated and over worked they call it quits. That's when champions are just getting started. You can call it "the second gear" or the "adrenalin kick" but that peak performance is what separates the good from the great. Winners can feel that second wind and actually outperform themselves each time they try harder. This builds confidence and self esteem in you. When your back is against the wall, winners meet the challenge and get beater each time. They don't quit.

The 4:00 Minute Mile

When you discuss peak performance and determination, there is no better lesson in sports than the breaking of the 4-minute mile. In the history of athletics, there was not a greater prize then to run a mile in less than four minutes. Runners were close. Some of the clocked times were 4:03.4 seconds but nobody could break that magical time of 4 minutes.

Breaking the four minute (4) mile at one time was considered impossible until Roger Bannister did it in Oxford, England on May 6, 1954. He ran the mile in under 4 minutes with a time of 3:59.4. Sir Roger was the first man to successfully run one-mile in less than 4 minutes. The sub-4:00 mile was now history. The impossible had been accomplished.

Now when track and field stars run the mile in less than 4 minutes it is considered almost routine. The last world record time was 3:43.9. A record once thought to be impossible to break is now broken on a routine basis. Not only are athletes running the mile faster but in incredible times. Nothing is impossible.

"The most rewarding things you do in life are often the ones that look like they can't be done."

—Arnold Palmer-Professional Golfer

In today's technological world, businessmen and entrepreneurs become millionaires overnight. Men and women in their early 30's are amassing huge amounts of wealth.

Why is that? Because people like Roger Bannister and these new millionaires share a dream. It could be an idea for a new product, making something better or improving your time in running the mile. How do they reach these goals? The answer is by personal determination and discipline.

After Sir Roger Bannister retired from track and field, he went back to college and became a Neurologist and later in life was the master at Oxford College. He retired in 2001. He was a champion on and off the track.

"I've missed more than 9,000 shots in my career. I've lost more than 300 games, and 26 times I've been trusted to take the game winning shot and missed. Throughout my life and career I've failed, and failed and failed again. And, that is why I succeed."

—Michael Jordan

Perseverance

If you want to achieve anything in life you must not quit. Even when your dreams are getting further away, rather than closer, don't give up. I fought in the Goodwill Games and represented the United

States. Sometimes what you are fighting for is bigger than you or me. Remember the Olympic spirit of one more round.

To succeed or win, you have to keep going, nothing is going to be easy. You must do what successful people do and that is to keep trying. You never really lose until you quit or stop trying. Most people give up just when they are about to achieve their goals.

It's like the treasure hunters who find sunken ships and recover millions of dollars in gold coins, jewelry, gold bars and other valuable artifacts. They dig and they dig but they never give up. There failure rate is 1000 to one but they just keep trying and eventually after one more dive, one more dig, they find the sunken treasure. How many times in your life were you close and just didn't know it?

> *Lance Armstrong who won the Tour de France seven times and was stripped of his titles after admitting to using performance enhancing drugs said it best: "Pain is temporary. It may last a minute, or an hour or a day, or a year, but eventually it will subside and something else will take its place. If I quit, however, it lasts forever."*

I really don't want to bash Lance here but there is a lesson to be learned from his experience. If you do something, do it right! Don't cut corners, or say, "well they are doing it also." You will never feel like a true champion if you know deep down inside that your victory was tainted. He must have felt some guilt all those years knowing that he cheated and won. I wish him luck and I know he will emerge a champion in other endeavors.

The German Olympic Champion and downhill skier Ingmar Stenmark was quoted after a race, "I would rather fall and not medal then take second place." That shows the determination for success from some Olympic athletes.

There Will Be Critics and Naysayers

My corporation started when I was ten (10) years old. I had the dream of becoming a professional boxer. People thought I was crazy and they would say, "You can't be the heavyweight champion of the world." Naysayer's are everywhere and ready to bring you down with their typical, "Are you crazy, you can't do that" attitude. Successful people don't pay attention to the naysayers or people with negative values.

> *"Optimism is the faith that leads to achievement. Nothing can be done without hope and confidence."*
>
> —*Helen Keller*

I'm going to give you some good advice. Move away from negative individuals. Find new friends. The old ones will drain the positive energy from you. Find a new group of friends. People who are like-minded and are always positive and action oriented. Find the group of people who look at the cup and always see the cup is half full and not half empty. This inspirational group wants to fill the cup up not drain it.

> *Confucius says:*
>
> *"Have no friends not equal to yourself."*

Surround yourself with friends and associates who will take you to the next level. Get away from the ones who are always saying, "It can't be done." Find new friends with the same vision you have. Work hard together and support each other no matter what their dream is. This champ says it best.

> *"It isn't the mountains ahead to climb that wears you out, it is the pebble in your shoe."*
>
> —*Muhammad Ali*

Believe In Yourself

When other people around you doubt your skills and your ability to win, that is the time when you must be at your peak performance. That is done by not just getting by but by performing above and beyond your normal abilities. You have to rise to the occasion.

Muhammad Ali was the king of believing in himself. He would talk you right out of a fight before it even started. The man made many believers when he knocked out the best fighters in the world. Remember, our lesson is to start believing that you can do it. It is a proven fact that you become what you think about most.

I would have enjoyed fighting Ali. As you know, I'm the quiet type with not a whole lot to say. It would have been fun to have Ali across the ring yelling at me and saying, "I'm going to beat you Michael Moorer because I'm the greatest. I'm gonna whoop you double M."

I was fighting Bert Cooper for the championship when he knocked me down in the fifth (5) round. I survived the round and got back to my corner and sat down. By the look in my trainers and managers eyes, they thought I was finished. There were very little words of encouragement except to just get through the next round. All of them thought the fight was over and I would not make it past the next round. They may have lost faith in me, but I didn't.

In this life, your life, it is a onetime event. Make the best of it. You have got to believe in yourself. When all others doubt you that is the time for you to excel.

"Our greatest glory is not in ever falling, but in rising every time we fall."

—*Confucius*

It's OK to be different

Every year, hundreds of new businesses open up, there are new artists and rock bands and most of them fail within two years. You might dream of opening a restaurant, an airline or a cleaning service. In business or the world of boxing the competition is relentless. To be successful you have to stand out in the crowd and offer something different. Do something that is not like everyone else. Try to be different. I was different because I fought south pay. Not many heavyweight boxers fought and trained that way.

Look at your competition and ask yourself, "What can I do better and offer more quality?" It's like a great movie. When you are finished and walking out of the theatre, you can't wait to tell someone about the film. It had the "Wow factor." Many people say that it can't be done anymore. There are already enough pizza fast food restaurants, chicken restaurants and computer companies that have captured the audience. I tend to disagree with them.

I know a guy who was a good mechanic and started driving to the customer to fix their vehicle rather than have the customer drive to his shop. Why, because successful people don't have four hours to sit and watch TV in an auto repair shop. His gift was he fixed the cars at night while the owner slept.

After one year he had three (3) trucks on the road and after the second year he had seven (7) trucks working around the clock. Something new, maybe? He did something different. He took the mechanic shop to the customer.

Specialization

Being different means you specialize in a skill that very few people can do. It could be a unique skill or specialty that very few people possess. That special skill could be that of a professional boxer, heart surgeon, computers, or even a language skill.

When you decide on a career, try to be original. The great motivational speaker Tony Robbins tells his students not to reinvent the wheel but just copy what your competition is doing. Tony calls it "modeling."

That does work and I agree with his philosophy up to a certain point. That will only take you so far because sooner or later you have to stand on your own merit and separate yourself from the rest of the crowd. Learn all you can and then just be true to yourself.

Recognizing the Problem

I don't care who you are or what you do, there will always be problems. It could be a difficult contract, performing at an outdoor concert and it's raining, being injured and try to finish the fight and more. The key is to tackle the problem head on, don't avoid it.

When you see it coming and don't take it seriously that's where the problem begins. It is easy to stop a lawsuit in the first stages of its legal development. Stopping it at the beginning is much easier than going to court two years later. Stop that law suit before it gets momentum. The closer it gets the stronger the momentum and the harder to block it or deflect the damage it will cause.

Whether you are a quarterback in the pocket, a boxer expecting a punch or a business person with employee problems, even though you know it was coming when it hits you, it will still rock your foundation.

It can affect an entire company from the top to the bottom. It can take the wind out of your sail just like a body punch. Every person or every ounce of your body will feel that punch and it will shake you to your core.

But sometimes you never see problems coming. The real shocker is when that problem hits you and you never saw it coming. Your stocks are up, profits are good and the future looks bright. Then suddenly your biggest and largest purchaser goes out of business. BAM!

It's like in a boxing match. You're feeling good, dancing like a butterfly; you're ahead on the score cards, then all of the sudden you're on your back staring up at the ring lights, wondering what the hell happened.

Las Vegas, 1994, I was fighting George Foreman and had him beat going into the 10th round. All the cards had me ahead and then from out of nowhere, he hits me with a right hand. Good night Irene! That would be my first loss as a professional boxer.

The best way to prepare for business problems is to prepare in advance. Keep your company fit, running on all eight cylinders, plug the holes and just keep moving forward. Companies must be physically fiscally and mentally fit. It's a long term commitment. The moment you company starts going backwards (declining cyclonic) it's difficult to recover whether you're a boxer or a business man.

> *"Each success only buys an admission ticket to a more difficult problem."*
>
> *—Henry Kissinger*

Don't Be Afraid of Failure

You are going to have some failure in your quest for success. That's OK as long as we learn from the experience. Let's look at failure from a different perspective. In baseball, the best hitters fail more than two thirds of the time. If you are batting over 333 that means you were called out 667 times. The best baseball players don't think about failure. Winners are not afraid of failing. On the other hand, losers never try because they are afraid of failure.

Moorer vs. Holyfield Rematch: Pride in Defeat

I did fight Evander Holyfield a second time after beating him in 1994. Our second fight was in November 1997. The fight was not that memorable except for the fact I lost. This fight was a turning point in my boxing career. We had not fought each other in three (3) years. When I fought Evander the second time he was ready for me.

My trainer was Freddie Roach. He told me that to beat Evander again I had to be at the top of my game. I needed to be faster, quicker and more evasive when he threw combinations at me. I had to be in the best physical shape of my life. It was going to be one hell of a fight. We both were hungry for the victory.

I had just beaten Botha and Schultz for the title. I regained the title when I out pointed Schultz on a 12 round split decision. Too close for comfort. I made sure there would be no decision when I fought Botha. I knocked him out in the 12th round with 18 seconds left in the fight. Both fights were extremely tough and may have taken away a little of my steam. I agreed to fight Evander again. The money was just too good to pass up.

The fight was at the University of Las Vegas campus and there were over 10,000 people in the stands. The fight started off good for me. I won the first three rounds. But after the third round I could tell that this was not the same Evander Holyfield I defeated three years ago.

This time he came for blood. His white trunks said, "Warrior" on the front. He came to take his title back. He just seemed quicker and his jab kept me off balance most of the fight. Tonight was going to be his night. This time he was ready for me.

The first time I went down was in the fifth round. He caught me with a combination and I hit the canvas. I was hurt but felt strong enough to weather the round and I did. I was in exceptional shape for this match and I thought it would go the distance. Our last fight went the full 12 rounds. My trainers and manager all believed this would be another tough fight and I would win it in the 12th round, I was wrong.

I felt good in the sixth round but the seventh was not my round. Evander started dancing and hit me with some bombs and I went down twice in this round. His upper cut and combinations were taking its toll. I could see the concern on Freddie's face.

After the fight doctor checked me he told the referee to stop the fight. The fight was stopped between the 8th and 9th round by Referee Mitch Halpern. I have never in my life been knocked down that many times. But each time he knocked me down, I got up. Bam, down I went and I kept getting up. Why, would I keep getting up? There is absolutely no way I am going to win the fight but each time I got up off the canvas. I was not going to quit. It's called pride. Pride in your profession and pride in yourself.

I wasn't quitting. I still thought I could win the fight if I got in close and hit him with a good left hand. I was not seeing what my trainers and my corner man were seeing.

The point is, I never gave up. Even getting knocked down five (5) times in 8 rounds I still felt as though I could win. Failure to me was not getting up. I may get beat but I'm not going to be counted out on my back. My training has always been to not give up and keep trying. This is what I am trying to convey to you the reader and that is perseverance. Don't ever quit. It will haunt you your entire life.

Remember I knocked out Botha with only 18 seconds left in the 12th round. Mentally I thought I was still in the Holyfield fight but physically I was finished. The ring doctor Flip Homansky stopped the fight after I couldn't respond to a question by Halpern.

There is a limit to how far your focus, determination and concentration can take you. Regardless, I gave it my best and I never quit. It was the fight doctor and the referee's decision to stop the fight, not mine. You know I hated to lose that fight but I didn't know until after the fight that Holyfield got $20 million and I got much less. It was a big fight and I should have been paid equally or more.

I have only lost four (4) times as a professional boxer. But, when I lost it really affected me. Not just for me but for each and every fan in the world that supported me and was in my corner. The fans that paid good money to see me win. The loyal fans who have been following my career for the past ten years. When you lose in boxing the loss is not only felt by you but the thousands of fans, promoters and friends around you. That is why it is so important to give it all you have every time you are asked to perform or shine.

Now, transition that into an acting career or a product that you make. They buy your product because they like it. If your customers stop liking the product, they will purchase it someplace else. Your customers and fans have an expectation from you and it is your job to deliver it.

Stay in the fight and don't quit. If you stop and give up you will never know how good it feels when you pull a victory out from the jaws of defeat. I was courageous that night and proud in my defeat.

Whatever you do in life, do it because you love it. It is important in your life to take pride in what you do. Boxers are warriors. In the ring it is combat and sometimes boxers are killed during the fight. I take my job seriously. You should also take your career seriously.

I don't care if you cut yards for a living or you are a barber. Take pride in your profession. I had so much respect for the sport of boxing I didn't want to just stay down and get counted out. I got up each time and tried. All you have to do in life is do your best and give it your maximum effort. Be proud and try. At least you can say, "I didn't quit."

"He who loses wealth loses much; He who loses a friend loses more; but he who loses courage loses all."

—Cervantes

One More Round

The United States Olympic Training Center (OTC) is located in Colorado Springs, Colorado. This is where a majority of our elite United States athletes train. At the OTC almost every sport is represented there. I trained there prior to the 1986 Goodwill Games and won a bronze medal for the USA.

Many of our elite athletes live and train at the OTC. It is a place where you have the time to dedicate your life to your sport. The athletes have a motto and it's written on most of the buildings at the OTC.

In the boxing pavilion the sign says, "One more round." In the swimming pool lobby the Olympic motivator sign says, "One more lap." That is how you get better. When you are completely tired, worn out and can't go anymore, that's when you don't quit. To be a champion or an Olympic Gold Medalist you have to go that extra round, or lap in the pool or dive. That is what separates the bronze medalists from the Gold medalists.

In life and sports it is amazing how many people quit when they are so close to finishing. If they had just enough perseverance to go that last mile they would have been successful.

> *"Victory belongs to the most persevering."*
>
> —*Napoleon Bonaparte - Emperor of France 1769-1821*

Key Points of Round 9: Perseverance

- Never Quit
- Sacrifice and sacrifice some more for success
- Nothing is impossible
- Don't be afraid to fail
- One more time

Progressive Action Steps (PAS)   Completed

1. Change your social group to like minded.   ☐

2. Be different   ☐

3. Meet problems head on   ☐

4. You can do it, one more round   ☐

5. I am getting stronger mentally and physically   ☐

6. I make my own decisions, not naysayer's   ☐

Notes

<u>ROUND 10</u>
Change

"Be the change you wish to see in the world"

—Gandhi

Change

As in life, boxing and business, things change. Your company or the boxer takes on an original style that works for awhile until your competition starts to copy you to learn how to defeat you. To continue winning you have to reinvent yourself. You have to always be moving forward with new ideas or learning different angles of throwing a punch. You must be creative. In boxing or business, you must change to what is current. That could be new training methods, nutrition, the media, pay per view television or trends just to name a few.

The economy changes, technology gets smarter and the corporate athlete or boxer must adapt. You either change or die. You have got to be current and aware of the environment surrounding you. An example would be;

If suddenly I stopped moving in a fight and just stand there, what do you think the other boxer is going to do? He is going to knock me out. I have got to keep moving and showing him punches he has never seen before. If my opponent hits me standing still he is going to give me the opportunity to show the pay per view television audience the proper technique for the canvas face plant, complete with one or more bounces. You must have positive movement and keep going forward.

Moving forward

To be successful and a winner in the business world you have to change. Concentrate on your personal development and grow each day. But most important you must keep moving forward and not backwards. Have you ever seen a boxer hit an opponent moving backwards? That's right; the punch has nothing behind it. Create change by moving forward and anticipate future economic trends and that left hook that comes out of nowhere. If you are constantly moving forward, you will never look back.

> *George Bernard Shaw stated, "Progress is impossible without change, and those who cannot change their minds, cannot change anything."*

Change is Constant

In this world, the only thing that is constant is change. In boxing, as in business things change. Stuff happens. "Where did that guy learn how to do that?" "That combination of punches wasn't in any of his first 10 fights!" He changed and learned something new.

A boxer must be constantly learning new punches. The same holds true for your company. New technology, computer graphics, or your hand held phone. It is Microsoft vs. Apple. Progress is moving forward with change, not going backwards. If you stop moving and learning each day, technology and economics will run you over.

Just like boxing, you must change with the times or prepare to be introduced to the canvas. In my line of work, if you don't think on your feet, you'll be thinking on your back. "Where did that come from, I never saw it coming." You are an entrepreneur open your eyes.

Create Change

What life path are you on? Do you take the left fork in the road or the right fork? If you take the wrong turn, it will change your life

126

forever. It's the very small moves like this in your life that will trigger the larger ones later in life. Sir Isaac Newton said "everything has a reaction."

When you finally make the decision to change, something has to go from your life. You don't have time to do everything you are doing now and have time for change. Let's look at your life as if it was a basket of fruit and you're changing your diet. Now the fruit basket is full of fruit that you may not like or can't eat. Some of it has to go.

The basket or your life can only hold so much. You may be busy but are you being productive. You have to take something out of the basket to make room to put something new in the basket. If you decide to start reading one hour a day that may mean you can't watch the Late Night Show before you go to bed. Hopefully we are taking out fruit that only interrupts your day and replacing it with fruit that will help you grow and change.

You have to look at your life as a journey across the ocean and you are the navigator. Don't let the boat just drift in the ocean. The winds and currents will take you in the direction they want to go. It is imperative that you take control and determine what direction your life/boat will go. When you don't control your life, you will end up at the exact spot you started at years ago. Create progressive change. What fruit in your basket are you going to take out and do without?

"Don't ask me what I did yesterday; ask me what I'm going to do tomorrow. That's what's important to me."

—*Michael Moorer*

Love and Hate

So far we have talked about changing because you want to do something you love. You may decide to change so you can buy that house, raise that family or get that new promotion. This change you make must be a positive step forward. That behavioral change is easier because now you have a goal. You want to buy a house. This change is easier because of the reward at the end.

You can change your life because you dislike something or love something. For example, let's just say, "Whaling in the pacific." You are against the commercial fishing of whales. You can quit work and go on a boat that attempts to save the whales. This change came out of something you didn't like that you wanted to change.

Our emotions can change our lives. The point is that change can occur due to you loving something or hating something. You will fight to change something you think is unfair. Either emotion can create change in your life. I referenced it only once in this book where I trained so hard because I didn't want to lose. Winning was important to me. It wasn't the fast cars, diamond jewelry, or big houses that pushed me to win every fight. It was the fear of losing. I just didn't want to lose. Fear, by itself, can be a motivator.

Computers and Information Technology

As a boxer, my career was a little before this technological time. But Olympic athletes today are using computers to learn how to train more efficiently. If you improve your training methods, you can perform at a higher level.

To be successful today you have got to be part of the computerized network. Everything you do in business will be affected by future technology. Whether you own a restaurant and see live video of your staff when you are on vacation or you own a trucking company where computers and I-pads calculate your payroll sheet, gas expenses or shipping manifest.

Don't stand there and just watch. Learn about computers, I-pads, lap tops, emails, Ebay and more. I just emailed a photo of boxing equipment I am having made in India. The manufacturer received it and now is making the equipment.

Computers are changing the way we do business on a daily basis. Learn the new technology or every one of your competitors will be out smarting you on a daily basis.

Change Is Not Easy

When I fought Evander Holyfield in 1994 for the heavyweight championship that was our first time ever fighting each other. I had a professional boxing record of 34-0 with 30 of those wins by knockout. Evander, known as "The Real Deal" had a record of 30-1. I was 26 years old and I had never been defeated. The current champ, Evander Holyfield, had lost only one fight. We both weighed in that night at 214 lbs. each. It was outdoors at Caesars Palace in Las Vegas. One of the commentators that night was George Foreman. It was going to be a great fight.

It was a slug fist from the first round, but I thought I was winning most of the rounds. He caught me with a good combination, I did go down in the fifth round, and that concerned my trainer. I was feeling pretty good about myself and thought, "If I just continue to do what I have been doing, I can beat this guy." My trainer, Teddy Atlas thought different.

Most people didn't even see it or realize what happened. After the seventh (7th) round, I went to my corner to sit down and Teddy Atlas blocks me from sitting down. He is standing in front of the stool. He's not letting me sit down in between this round. Teddy yells at me and says, "You don't need the chair unless you are going to listen to me." I was not doing what he wanted me to do during each round. He wanted me to change from what I was doing.

I thought I was doing great after getting knocked down in the 2nd round, but my trainer had a different plan. He wanted me to do more than what I was doing. Throw more combinations, an overhand left hand and maybe an upper cut then go to the head. He wanted me to change but I thought I was doing great.

That night George Foreman was one of the fight announcers. I was told that George said, "Michael has got to fight the full round." I guess I wasn't doing enough. I'm standing there tired and Teddy Atlas finally lets me sit down on the ring stool and starts yelling at me. "Don't come back if you don't win this round." In the end he was correct and I followed his lead and won the fight.

"Men marry women with the hope they will never change. Women marry men with the hope they will change. Invariably they are both disappointed."

—Albert Einstein

Southpaw to Orthodox

Occasionally you will see boxers change from their original fighting stance or style. They are either fighting orthodox or southpaw. What that means is they will put the right foot our front on the left foot and fight from that stance. They will change their stance and fight from a different boxing position. This is done to confuse their opponent and at the same time give you a chance to beat your opponent to the punch by doing something different.

You see it all the time. A new comedian on television will have a different persona than anyone else. He or she is different and it works for a while. But if they fail to change they are destined to be unemployed in the future. Think about this approach when you apply for a job, write a book or perform as a comedian. Sometimes change is good.

The Competition

Every year, thousands of entrepreneurs open up new businesses from restaurants to real estate offices. Most of them are out of business and have failed within two years. Those thousands of people dreamed of being successful and have lost all or most of their savings. Many of them failed because they did not look at their competition.

In the world of boxing or business, the competition is relentless. To be successful, you have to stand out in the crowd and offer something different. You have to offer something the competition doesn't have. I was different because I fought southpaw. Not many heavyweight boxers were trained that way. I was the only heavyweight in history to win the championship-fighting southpaw.

Know Your Competition

It is crucial to your survival to know your competition or opponent. I don't just take a fight and show up. Prior to getting into the ring I have done extensive home work on my competition. Who is your opponent or competition? What is your opponent or competition doing? What are they doing that makes them successful?

Hundreds of business professionals have a vision and open a business without ever researching their competition or the market. I moved through three different weight classes to become the world heavyweight champion. I fought light heavyweight and middle weight before moving to the heavyweight division. Before I moved to a different weight class, I looked at the competition and evaluated my chances of beating the ranked boxer(s).

Companies have to do the same. My skills, work ethic and physical strength grew as I learned the business of boxing. I just didn't move from division to division. I studied my competition before I moved up into a higher weight class. If you open a restaurant, you had better know your competition prior to opening. Don't move to a different division without researching your chances of success. A successful person knows the competition.

Protect Yourself at All Times

When a boxing match begins the referee will always say to both fighters, "Protect yourself at all times." In business and as a manager those five words should be your daily mantra. Protect myself at all times.

Every day as a business person or a professional, you have to stand guard all the time. Not part of the time but all the time. Why, because someone you know, a "friend" or a competitor wants to destroy you. Yes, that is right. They want to see you go out of business. It could be a current employee, an ex-employee, business associate or a customer. One or all of them want to see you and your company fail. It may be just competitive jealousy of just plain greed. Rest assure they would like nothing better than to knock you and your company out.

How can someone take your business down? Let's just look at one or two examples. How about sexual harassment? One of your employees approaches another employee or customer and says something sexual or derogatory and bam, you have a law suit. How do you defend against this? You protect yourself by writing, implementing and enforcing a companywide sexual harassment protocol.

As a fighter I have gotten hit below the belt, head butted, punched after the bell and hit with illegal rabbit punches. Anyone of these illegal punches can cause cuts, shut down my nervous system or damage an internal organ. The funny thing is that my opponent does this when there are millions of people watching. He hopes the ring referee will not see it.

Look what Tyson did to Evander Holyfield. He bit his ear off. Tyson states that Evander was head butting him and the referee did nothing about it. The referee didn't do anything so Mike bit off Evander's ear and spit it out on the ring canvas. So I have to protect myself at all times. Remember that is what the ring referee tells us at the beginning of the fight. That is your first mantra as a business professional.

Do you think that your competition follows all the rules in business? You don't think a boxer, if he can, get in a cheap shot he won't take it. Hell yes he will do it. Many of your competitors would love to see you down for the count or you fail. Why, because they want what you have. They truly believe that you do not deserve your success. It's just Mother Nature but you will find one day that one or two of your friends want you to lose.

It is always important to protect yourself and your company at all time. You protect yourself by issuing corporate rules and regulations, standard operating procedures, having good insurance, employee-training programs etc. If you do not protect yourself, your competition will find your weakness and use it against you. They will find that chink in your armor. Protect yourself at all times. That is what we do in boxing because the competition is ruthless.

Picking up the Pieces

I don't care what career you are in or you are dieting trying to lose weight there will be setbacks. Employees are people and people get sick and die. Equipment breaks down and now you have to go out and borrow money to keep your equipment going to continue to make money. It is the same problem in boxing.

During my career, my equipment broke down and had to be repaired. Here is a list of my injuries and surgeries during my boxing career.

- 4 surgeries on my left hand
- 1 surgery on my right hand
- 1 on my right wrist
- 2 on my right elbow
- 4 major surgeries on my right shoulder
- 2 on my left shoulder

- 1 left knee
- 2 surgeries on my right knee

That is a total of 17 surgeries on my body so I could continue to work. Many of the pro NFL athletes have more than 4 or 5 surgeries during their career. Like your business, the equipment breaks down and has to be fixed.

What is the secret? Get it fixed as fast as possible and get back in the race. You are not making money sitting at home when a $100,000 piece of equipment is sitting idle waiting to be repaired.

Financially: Live Within Your Income

You have seen it a hundred times in business professionals, actors, and boxers. They go from rags to riches and back to rags. I have won a lot of money during my career and spent most of it. We tend to believe the gravy train will not stop. But it does. Like George Foreman, I am reaching out and making money in the business world after my boxing career.

Look at some of the greatest boxers in history and many of them can't rub two quarters together. I made millions fighting Holyfield and Foreman and spent millions shortly thereafter. As successful individuals this has got to stop. Save some of the money you make.

This chapter is about change. In business or your profession we can make a lot of money fast and then nothing for a few years. We have to budget ourselves for the lean years. This is easier said than done. The key is to live within your means.

The NFL or the National Football League does it right. They have a financial organization that consults with their rookies and new draft choices. These rookie kids go from zero income in college to making 4 to 5 million dollars their first year as a pro and they are guaranteed another 20 million over the next few years. The NFL also has a retirement program for veterans who play more than 7 years. Boxing doesn't have a 401 K plan. Does your corporation or family plan have a retirement program?

The key is to spend less than you make and save 10% of what you make for an emergency fund. This is nothing new. All of the success managers recommend this to all of the people who achieve financial success after struggling for so many years. Spend some and save some and your future will be bright.

"The question isn't what age I want to retire, it's at what income."

—*George Foreman*

Never Underestimate Your Opponent

These little jewels of advice have been tested throughout time. I just didn't just make this up for the book. In this chapter or round it is "Never underestimate your opponent." The key is never being overly confident and always expect the unexpected.

Here I am at the peak of my boxing career. I have never lost a professional boxing match in my life. I'm fighting for the heavyweight championship of the world and the score cards have me way ahead. Big George Foreman is tired and just about out of steam. All I have to do is get through the next nine minutes or three rounds of the fight and I will unify the heavyweight championship and belts. I'm on easy street.

Remember the axiom, the master teaches his students all they know but not all he knows. I should have known better. George Foreman was the master and I was the student. Old age and treachery will always beat youth and skill. George lulled me into slowing down, just a little, and then he hit me. Goodnight Irene and the rest is history.

In business, war, divorce and boxing never underestimate your opponent. If you drop your guard for one minute it will change your history forever.

Life Changes

In life and boxing you hope you are still standing in the later rounds. Life and boxing do parallel each other. In life or the first few rounds of a fight you are full of energy, life is good, you're dancing and then the later rounds come around.

Rounds seven, eight and nine are the difficult years in life. You're in your forties and you're working your tail off to impress the judges.

You never got that winning lotto ticket or that quick knockout. Now you have to work extremely hard just to survive.

The last three rounds are the toughest. You are tired but still motivated. Your body hurts but you are still fighting. You are trying to win the last few rounds so you can win at life. But the only problem is your opponent is not helping. He doesn't care about old age, house payments, college tuition for the kids, IRS taxes, or trying to save for your retirement fund. All this is pulling most of your energy away. Forget the lotto. If it hasn't happened by now it probably won't happen.

So you work extra hard those last few rounds and even a little more. When the fight is over life's judges will be there and they will ask you, do you deserve to win? Have you done your best? Were you an honest competitor and a respected man or woman? Why should I pick you over your opponent? Did you prepare yourself for the later rounds in life?

So it all comes down to planning, working hard, being honest and doing your very best. If you have done all that and more, just maybe the score card of life will be in your favor.

You Can't Always Be the Champ: Adjusting to Change

In business and your career you have to adjust to changes. It is just the way that life cycles. Sometimes business is great and other times the economy is bad and it is difficult making a dollar. The key is you have to be flexible and work your way through adverse times.

During my championship years, life was good. The "Champ is in the house." Everywhere I went people treated me better than I could have imagined. Free drinks, football and baseball tickets, beautiful women, pictures, free clothes, meeting other celebrities, it was great. But, when you lose that title everything changes.

I am really a very quiet and soft spoken individual. I don't yell or get too excited. If you knew me you would probably say I am an introvert. Someone who likes to be left alone and probably wouldn't speak to you unless you started the conversation. I am very reserved and timid until I got into the ring.

In the boxing ring it is show time. It's like you turned on a switch and told me, "Michael it's time to go to work." I'm there working in the ring. I'm probably a lot like professional football players. The offensive linemen are usually quiet guys until the ball is snapped and then they turn into raging bulls. The whistle blows, the switch is turned off and they are mild again. It really is a great mix if you know how to turn it off and turn it back on.

In life, our bodies change but mentally I'm still the young boxer trying to get to the top again. You feel as though you can still do it but your body is just a few seconds behind where you really need it to be. You can change your physique but it is difficult to change your mind.

Who are you?

At the end of your life you will find that three things are important:

1. It is <u>not</u> important what you have.
2. It is <u>not</u> important what you have done.
3. What is important is <u>who you are</u>.

An example would be an infamous great leader who wrote books, conquered entire continents, developed his country into a world power and inspired millions of people. Who might this person be? His name would be Adolf Hitler. This ruthless tyrant killed millions of people. With his personal power and intelligence (one might also call it madness) he could have been a great leader. In the end he was one of the most ruthless and evil men of our time.

In the end you will be judged by many and you might not care. But, what is most important is how you see yourself and what you did during your life. Try to be that person that shares and gives no matter what your financial situation is. Live your life to the max. Do what you want to do and not what others want you to do. You have control over your life. At the end of the day or your life you can look yourself in the mirror and say, "I'm good with what I did during my life."

Look in the mirror and ask yourself, "Who am I?" Then ask yourself, "Do I like what I see in the mirror?"

You don't have much time to make the changes. Always feel good about yourself and your life will change dramatically. If you can't love yourself than how can you love someone else?

Change begins with a dream

John F. Kennedy our 42nd President challenged the United States and changed the world. He boldly stated to the United States Congress in 1961, "I believe that this nation should commit itself to achieving the goal, before this decade is out, of landing a man on the Moon and returning him safely to the Earth. The United States will go to the moon not because it is easy but because it is hard." On July 26, 1969, Apollo 11 Astronaut Eugene Edwin Buz Aldrin Jr. walked on the moon for the first time in history.

Kennedy was a visionary who looked at the world and tried to create change during his tenure as President. Unfortunately, he was killed in Dallas, Texas on November 22, 1963 by Lee Harvey Oswald. His visions were lost in time when he was assassinated.

"Some men see things as they are and say, "why?" I dream things that never were and say, "Why not?"

—John F. Kennedy-35th President of the United States.

Have a plan and create change in your life. You can be anyone you want to be. Just go out and do it.

Focus on Important Tasks

You can work all day and accomplish a lot of tasks but never get anything completed. Ever have those days where you worked incessantly all day and nothing got done. To prevent these unproductive days from occurring the key is to prioritize important tasks and get them done first.

Secondly, don't take the easy road in the morning. The morning is the best time for you to start that new project you have been putting off for weeks. You will find that once you get moving you will have more energy and motivation in the morning hours. When the day ends you will look back and see that you were productive and things got done.

Before you start your day sit down and prioritize what is important to get accomplished. Write down the ten (10) things you want to get done. Remember the Greek mantra, "Carpe Diem". It means seize the day. Make this, one of those days where you just get stuff done. You will find that your ability to prioritize the important and unimportant is one of the keys to success in life and your work.

Zig Ziglar the inspirational motivational speaker teaches that everyday should be treated, as that day before you go on vacation. Did you ever plan a vacation and the day before you leave you accomplish so many things. At the end of the day you look back and say to yourself, "What a great day, I got a lot accomplished before we leave tomorrow." Don't be afraid of hard work. It is the only way anything ever gets done.

"It is only through labor and painful effort, by grim energy and resolute courage that we move on and get on to better things."

—Eleanor Roosevelt

Change the Easy Way

Here is the easiest way to change your life. Start reading books. In the morning when you get the daily newspaper don't pick it up and immediately go to the sports section to see if I won my fight last night. My boxing history will not change your life. The only life it changes is mine or my opponent. I want you to read the business section first. The economy will have a far greater effect on your life than my boxing record.

Start reading books on business, computers, and financial periodicals. I also recommend books on motivational or inspirational books. After two years (that seems to be the magic time table for your life to change) you will notice a difference. Your friends will change; you will be more intelligent, think clearer and better. Hopefully you move to a new career that challenges you and creates advancement in your life.

Change by Modeling

Did you ever hear the term, "you don't have to reinvent the wheel?" You can copy something and still be successful. One way to change is through modeling. Copy something you like.

Copy someone who is a winner and that you look up to.

I want you to find someone, a role model for you to imitate. Then with or without their permission you model your behavior, mannerisms, and life style after theirs. What did you just say? Yes, you heard it right. Become that person. This is called modeling.

You will never copy that person exactly but you will pick up several of their best qualities or traits. Maybe they dress like a winner or carry themselves in public just a little different than most people.

If they are a winner it's because of something they have or do. That person may have the "X" factor or maybe just an abundance of confidence. Maybe that "something" could help you become a better person. That "X" factor they have, you may not have. But, maybe you can learn from them how to duplicate that behavior for yourself.

A boxing example would be for me to copy Mike Tyson's uppercut. It works for Mike, maybe it would work for me. It is a simple as that.

A friend of mine named Dan, actually took on the persona of James Bond. He started dressing like Bond, began taking martial arts lessons, started smoking a pipe, and drank only Martinis shaken not stirred. Dan also purchased an Austin Martin vehicle just like James Bond. He went on to become a very successful private investigator. He currently travels the world doing cases for the very wealthy. It worked for him.

Create Change While You Drive

We talked about it earlier in a previous round. It is time to go out and purchase a motivational CD and play it going to work every day. Turn the radio off and start VAL or Vehicle Audio Learning. When you know that CD by heart and have implemented some of the suggestions go out and buy a second CD on another inspirational topic. There are hundreds of motivational tapes and discs that can help you.

This is by far one of the easiest ways for personal change. You will not change the first month but I can assure you, if you keep listening to the tapes and applying some of the principles, you will change and be a more productive person. Keep learning. There is always someone who can teach you something.

Your Time Is Valuable

Motivational speaker Jim Rohm once said, "Time is more valuable than money. You can get more money, but you cannot get more time."

Management of your time is imperative to success. There will come a day in your successful career when it is cheaper to hire some else to do some of your work for you. You have become a valuable asset to your company and your time is limited. What tasks or duties did you do today that consumed your time and really didn't bring in any income?

The tasks we talk about could be something as simple as driving, making dinner, washing the car, going through emails or even going through corporate mail. Time is money. It is important to maximize your time so you can make more money. Now you can spend that four or five hours a week doing something productive.

Here is a quick story on lost time. A friend of mine owns a gun store and an investigative agency. He has been in business for over 20 years and has become a good businessman. He runs a pretty tight ship and is always trying to maximize his profits. He will not hire anyone now who smokes. This is kind of funny but in reality he is right.

One day he said to me, "If that employee goes outside and smokes a cigarette five (5) times a day, that is lost corporate time. If you take the average time it takes for that person to smoke a cigarette is about 4-5 minutes. Figure it out. Five cigarettes a day and let's say 4 minutes each. That is 20 minutes a day of lost time. Five days a week at 20 minutes is how much time? Each week that is 100 minutes or one hour and 40 minutes of unproductive time. Now calculate one year or 52 weeks. In the end you will find the employee spent 86 hours or two weeks of corporate time during the year "taking a break outside for 5 minutes smoking." Don't waste your time doing non-productive activities.

Key Points of Round 10: Change

- Change forward
- Know your competition
- Never under estimate your opponent-adversary
- Your time is valuable, don't waste it
- Modeling might get me over the hump

Progressive Action Steps (PAS)   Completed

1. Buy motivational tapes   ☐

2. Start changing today-slowly   ☐

3. Today I made one modeling change   ☐

4. I come home now and work on my future   ☐

5. I have started to take better care of myself   ☐

Notes

ROUND 11
Timing

"There is nothing more powerful than an idea whose time has come."

—Victor Hugo

Timing Is Everything

Success is about timing. Knowing when to make that move or to take action or not take action. Timing many times is the number one factor for success or failure. Timing is important if you're a professional gambler, comedian who tells jokes, race car driver, movie producer releasing a movie, or a manufacturer of toys. You have to take action when the time is right.

I was fighting Botha for the world heavyweight championship. The opportunity to knock him out was there. He was open for a right jab and then a left hook combination because he kept dropping his left hand. We were running out of time. It was the last round and I needed to impress the judges at the end of the fight.

So I waited and planned for just those punches. I was timing myself when that window of opportunity presented itself. It was timing that would put me in the right place at the right time. I had prepared myself for this moment my entire life. There it is, I hit him with every molecule in my body and down he went. He didn't get up and we had a winner.

There's the story, now here is the point. When an opportunity presents itself to you or your company, you have to be in a position to recognize it and take advantage of it. It's called timing, being at the right place at the right time.

The Pulse of Your Corporation

As a professional athlete I know my body. I have taken very few fights when I wasn't a fined tuned instrument and running on all eight cylinders. The same philosophy happens in your business. It's physical and psychological and as a business owner you can feel it. You know when your corporation is not running as it should.

After a few years, your business or corporation becomes a living and breathing organization. You can feel when it's running smooth and know when it's hurting. The pulse of your corporation will decide your corporate health. As the leader or owner of the company you will feel this and know when the timing is right. Some people call it instinct.

This feeling or instinct is 3 billion years old. Many executives and professionals have listened to their gut feeling and made the right decision. This is one of your six senses that tells you something is wrong or right. Do not disregard this little voice in your head.

"If a man writes a better book, preaches a better sermon, or makes a better mousetrap than his neighbor, the world will make a beaten path to his door."

—*Ralph Waldo Emerson*

Take what's there and Work With It

When I'm in the ring fighting my opponent spends about half of his time covering up so I can't hit him. He knows I throw a mean left hand so he's protecting that area of his body. I have to take what he gives me and work with it.

I can't hit him with my best shot so I have to adapt to the situation and work with what is available. The key is, whatever they give you put some power behind it. I can't hit him in the head or jaw but his ribs and kidneys are there. Bam, Bam, Bam, take it and put some extra punch in it. Take advantage of that small window of opportunity. You know what I do? I put every ounce of power I have in the kidney punch and guess what happens. After a while it begins to work. I'm winning and the punches are taking its toll.

It's the exact same philosophy in business. It may be your location, time of the year or the products you sell. Whatever, it doesn't matter. Nevertheless, what you have to do is take what the market gives you. The key is maximizing what you doing.

Career Example

A good analogy would be acting. You are an actor and have gotten a few parts but it's been slow. You are offered a small part in a big movie. The question is do I take what is offered or hold out for a larger movie contract offer? Take what is offered and maximize that small part. It could open doors for you. It may build into a larger more attractive contract in the future.

It's just like boxing. The body shots don't take effect until later in the rounds. The key is to stay in the fight. If you did not take that small movie part, you might not be offered anything for a long time.

Time

Of all the things you can buy or purchase, time is not one of them. Your time is extremely valuable. You are given only so many hours on this earth and they are rapidly being depleted. Savor and conserve your valuable hours each day.

Don't waste your time. The star or actor Rocky Balboa or Sylvester Stallone is known for getting things done and not wasting valuable time. Do you know why? Sly has calculated how many hours he has to live. He doesn't waste time.

He has calculated that in a year there are only 8,760 hours. If you think about that, it's not that many. Check this out. The next 20 years has only 175,200 hours total. If you think about your life and time like that, it's really not a whole lot of time. Don't waste it. Get started on your success now.

Did you ever notice that people who have nothing to do always want to spend their time with you? This kills your productive genes for that day. I usually give them a few minutes and then move on to what I was doing before they got there. It's not how many hours you work in a day but what you accomplished during those hours.

Time Off

After losing to Foreman I have to say I was a little shocked. That was my first professional career loss. Not only did I lose but I got knocked out while the world watched. I was a heavy favorite to win the fight. I had the fight won if I could have moved around a little more and just finished the last three rounds. I have to give George credit. He reached down deep and pulled victory from defeat. It was a humbling experience. I needed some time off to regroup. I just needed personal time to reflect and be by myself. Sometimes down time is good time.

I came back strong 2 years later and fought Alex Schultz in the Westfalen Stadium in Germany. He was German and this was his country. Let's just say it was a tough crowd. We were fighting for the IBF or International Boxing Federation title. I won that night by a split decision. It felt good to win the World Heavyweight title again even if it was just part of it. There is the WBA title and a few more out there.

Expect the Unexpected

Most business deals start out slow and after a while accelerate to a good pace and you are on track. The first few meetings are "feeling out the other person." The same thing happens in boxing, sometimes.

When you watch most boxing matches the boxers come out and the during the first round or second round not much happens. I'm watching my opponent, getting his timing down and getting a feel for his power and movement. I'm feeling out my opponent. When the third round rings normally I'm rocking. That is if there is a third round.

In business and boxing you should expect the unexpected from your competitor. Right now in the economy Burger King is making all of their restaurants sell a double cheeseburger for $1.00.

The restaurant loses money on every sale. Now McDonalds and Pizza Hut are trying to catch up. Burger King did the unexpected. A dollar for a double hamburger with cheese, are you kidding me?

If your competitor does the unexpected, it is important that you weather the storm until you can catch up. Don't do anything drastic, just cover up and plan an offensive campaign for your company. That is what I should have done when I fought David Tua at the Trump Taj Mahal in Atlantic City in 2002.

Always be Prepared

I'm scheduled to fight David Tua. He is an up and coming fighter with an unusual style but should be a good start for my come back. It's not.

The bell rings and I am expecting us to go to the center of the ring, maybe touch gloves and get this show on the road. He does the unexpected. When the bell rings Tua runs across the ring to my corner and really surprised me. Out of nowhere he catches me with a right hand. He hits me about 20 times in less than 30 seconds. I do the best I can to recover but it's not going to happen. He knocks me out in 30 seconds of the first round. He did the unexpected.

In business, football, investing, love and every other part of your life, expect the unexpected. Plan for that and you will never get caught off guard. The unexpected could be a 50 yard touchdown pass on first down, your wife serving you with divorce papers or the stock market diving to a new low. You must plan for the unexpected.

You and I have no control over so many things in our lives. But some things we can control. Think outside the box and try to have a plan for every part of your life. Control the things you can. It is your life and only you can control it.

Analyze Your Failures

Whatever happens you are responsible for the results. Take responsibility for your actions. In boxing, it's not the ring judge's fault and they gave me a raw deal. It's not the director's fault for cutting me from the movie and it's not the economy's fault why my business failed. It's your fault. Own up to being responsible for your actions.

If you would have done that it may have solved the problem and the result may be different. Analyze what happened and not why it happened.

That is the beauty of instant replay on TV today. I get to watch myself getting knocked out time and time again. And now it's year to year. Do you know how many times I have seen George Foreman knocking me out? That's OK because I learn from my mistakes. When you fail, sit down and analyze what happened and take steps to correct it. Don't let things happen, make it happen, so you can control the end results. Make the results favorable to you.

We all hate to fail. But failure is only if you quit after being defeated. I boxed after Tua cleaned my clock. I didn't stop because boxing was something I loved doing. Hundreds of companies have been on the brink of bankruptcy and didn't quit. They looked at their mistakes and took corrective action to get back on top.

As for me, never again will a boxer charge me from across the ring and embarrass me on national television. That's the last time that will ever happened. I learned from my mistake and continued being successful.

It's Time to Shine

As a pugilist, only a few boxers reach the top. After years of hard work, a ten year plan and thousands of hours of training, if you are good and a little lucky you might get ranked in the top ten.

If I'm fighting to retain my championship belt or you finally saved enough money to open your own restaurant, you will have one chance to impress the judges. You will have one chance to shine, make it count.

What do I mean? You have the opportunity to make it. You have invested all of your money into this restaurant, your corporation or career and now your finally get the opportunity to show what you are made of. You cannot fail. You must light up like a light bulb.

What separates the good from the great? There are hundreds of good actors that never make it. There are hundreds of good business executives that are captured in a small company and just can't get that break. Then there is the boxer that has all the skills but just lacks that "X" factor.

What separates the good from the great, that little extra effort and skill? That little extra effort can make you shine. This is the one chance to show everybody that you deserve to be where you are. A lot of people doubted you and said you couldn't do it. But now is the time to for you to prove them wrong. Be confident. You know that you can do it. It is your moment in time. Make it count.

"The temptation for greatness is the biggest drug in the world."

—*Mike Tyson*

Don't Always Look for the Big Shot

It would be nice in life to begin a career and hit it big your first year. That normally doesn't happen. If you start a business today, you will probably not make money for at least 2 years. It is the same in boxing. Everyone is looking for the big shot, the knockout punch or the home run. Those do not come around that often. You will find out that you have to work for that opportunity.

It will take a lot of rounds to win most boxing matches. It is the same in business. Not many people start a business and strike it rich the first year. You have to work very hard for that first big win.

Take Time Out

In business or when you are climbing to the top, it is important to take time out. Many busy executives will go away for a weekend rather than take a full week off. Those 2 or 3 short days recharges their batteries and after being gone only 2 days, they are roaring to go in on Monday morning. You body, mind and soul needs a rest.

In between rounds I get one minute to rest. The first thing I do is try to control my breathing. Once I have that under control, I then listen to my corner men. The point is that everyone needs to take a minute or time off to regroup and get back in the fight.

I use to feel guilty when I took a day off from training prior to a big fight. My trainers would go crazy. Why did I take that day off because my body was telling me, "Michael we need a little time to rest." Listen to your body. A good example of that are infant children. They will reject some foods but eat other foods. At 6 months old they know exactly what foods their body needs to grow. Your body will tell you what it needs, if you just take the time to listen.

"Do you love life? Then do not squander time, for that's the stuff life is made of."

—*Benjamin Franklin*

Every Round Counts and So Does Every Customer

Businesses and boxing both have momentum. If you lose a round in boxing the other fighter gains momentum. He comes out with more confidence and determination to put you away. It is the same in business.

Every round counts in boxing and every customer counts. You build a business one customer at a time or win one round at a time. The score card in boxing is your customer satisfaction. If the customer likes the business they will return. If the score card is in your favor you will win.

You can't take a round off in boxing and win the fight. It is the same in business if you decided one day just to shut the door and close down for the day. You build a customer base and a following. Every day or every round in boxing counts.

"Being deeply loved by someone gives you strength; loving someone deeply gives you courage."

—*Lao –Tzu*

Key Points of Round 11: Timing

- Timing is everything
- Always be prepared
- It's Ok to take time off
- Listen to your instincts
- Expect the unexpected

Progressive Action Steps (PAS)   Completed

1. Take time out to relax   ☐

2. When the time is right shine   ☐

3. Keep the momentum going   ☐

4. I worked hard today to improve my life   ☐

ROUND 12
Fighting for Success

"Nothing is worth more than this day."

—Goethe

What Is Your Purpose In Life?

Did you ever wonder what separates winners from losers? Why some people prevail and others fail. Is it because they are smarter, better educated, great looks, or are born with the golden spoon in their mouth? No, those are not the answers. The answer is that successful people and winners have an instinctive internal feeling. It is as if they have a calling in life. They are born with a burning drive and a mission to accomplish more during their lifetime. They do not settle for mediocrity. The react and follow their instincts. Winners say this feeling is hard to explain.

Not everyone has this feeling of "Greatness." Some people know it is there and do nothing with it. While others who achieve success acknowledge the instinctive drive and do something about it. They act on their gut feeling. You can think about it your entire life but nothing changes until you decide to challenge yourself and follow your instincts.

One day you will make that burning decision to change your life. Many of the winners do not know what it is until late in life but they just have this feeling that they have been put on this earth for a higher purpose. What is your purpose in life?

"Discipline is doing what you hate to do, but nonetheless doing it like you love it."

—*Mike Tyson- Former Heavyweight Boxing Champion of the world*

Foundation for Success

When you build a house or a tall building what is the first thing the construction engineer does. He designs, plans and builds a foundation of strength to support the new house or tall building. The same principle should apply to you when you are building.

If you have the love and support at home, your life will be stronger. Can you imagine the construction engineer building that sky scraper? He or she fears that at any moment it could collapse. That's you at home. When you leave the house in the morning it should be the rock or foundation of your life. Because in reality whatever you do affects your family at home. That is why it is so important that your family supports your goals. If your goals are shared, everyone wins.

Financial Success?

You see it way to often where a well known boxer files for bankruptcy. They made tens of millions of dollars and now they are broke. Why is that? They fought their entire lives for success and finally reached it and now they have no money.

Byron Campbell has been training boxers and in the fight business for over twenty-five years. He recently told me that 99% of the boxers who have no money at the end of thier professional career is due to poor money management. In many cases it is not the boxer who mismanaged the money but someone in a position of trust. Basically they get ripped off by a friend, family member or the person they trusted to manage thier money.

They make the mistake of trusting a family member or someone who came highly recommended to them and put too much trust in that person to manage their money and financial affairs. The mantra for a boxer today is D.T.A. Don't Trust Anyone.

Campbell went on to say that the smart boxers who retired finacially secure did one of two things. First, most of them personally managed and invested their own money. If they lost thier money it was thier fault and no one else. Secondly boxers who retired with money were actively involved with thier financial team. The financial advisor would make recommendations and they would decide where the money was spent. The key is to thier success was to be actively involved in the management of thier money.

Fighting for Success

If you want to be a winner and become successful, you will have to fight to reach the top. Nobody is going to give you anything. Then once you are successful a new battle begins. That is trying to remain at the top. After beating Holyfield I was scheduled to fight Foreman. The boxing commission actually tells fighters who they have to fight. If you don't fight they take away the title and it becomes vacant. You are forced to defend your title.

Business or boxing is not for the faint hearted. You are going to get hit with low blows, dishonesty, bad decisions, money problems and numerous other issues. Buckle up your seat belt because it's going to be a rocky journey.

Winning and being successful is a habit. Like one of the NFL coach stated during a press conference, "We play to win the game." If winning didn't matter then no one would be keeping the score. Learn to be a winner. Expect to win. Fight to win. Start today in becoming a winner. Remember, in boxing and in life, there is no second place.

Life is made up of moments. The easy ones are not that important. It is the hard ones that really count. Vince Lombardi the Green Bay Packers football coach talks about victory and he said, " That he firmly believes that any man's finest hour, the greatest fulfillment of all that he holds dear, is that moment when he has worked his heart out in a good cause and lies exhausted on the field of battle – victorious."

I had that feeling when I beat Holyfield for the championship. It is a moment I will never forget. If you ever see the fight tapes I do show some emotion that night. You will have to fight for success but when it arrives, it is worth it.

"I am a Shawnee. My forefathers were warriors. Their son is a warrior. From my tribe I take nothing. I am the maker of my own fortune.

—*Tecumeseh- He was the leader of the Shawnee Indians.*

Knowing That You Found Success

How will you know when you have found success? Is it when I buy my first new car or I buy a condominium on Miami Beach? That sounds like success but I am not really sure.

You will recognize it immediately. How, when you are content with your life. When you give love and are loved. The love comes from your family, friends and your job.

You are healthy financially and physically. You know that your family is being taken care of and they need very little. You are healthy and exercise to keep fit. You feel secure at work knowing that 1) You are doing a good job 2) Knowing your company is financially healthy and 3) Employees and associates care about you.

Again, the key to success is balancing your obligations with your personal needs. If you can do that successfully then you have arrived at where you wanted to be when you started years ago. Relax and enjoy it.

"It doesn't matter if it's boxing or business. It is still a fight for survival. The person who has the strongest determination and the best skills will prevail."

—*Michael Moorer*

How Much Is Enough?

It is reported that I made 22 million dollars during my boxing career. I really never looked at my finances until I needed money. Then I would just ask for it and I got what I needed for that day. I do know I made 5 million dollars fighting Evander the first time and 8 million dollars the second time. My biggest payday ever was losing to George Foreman. I made 10 million dollars for that fight. We discussed a rematch but it never happened. The money you make is relative to the money you spend.

So how much money, cars, houses, jewelry, and stuff do you need? Do you know what the funny part is, that you can only drive one car at a time, live in one house at a time and only wear one watch at a time. The secret is to make enough money so you can save enough money. I will repeat that, make a lot of money and save part of it. Spend a lot but save some. The rest of the money is all fluff.

> *Muhammad Ali had a philosophy about success and wealth. He said, "To be able to give away riches is mandatory if you wish to possess them. This is the only way that you will truly be rich."*

I was at a Police PBA versus Firefighters boxing match one night and Angelo Dundee was there. Dundee was Ali's trainer for most of his career. We were sitting there watching police officers and firefighters doing the best they could to hit each other. We started talking and Angelo started telling Muhammad Ali stories. The quote above by Ali is absolutely truthful.

He told me that if you liked the watch that Ali was wearing and made a comment like, "Hey, nice watch." Ali would take the watch off and give it to you. He didn't care if the watch was worth $1000 dollars or $50,000 dollars. He would just take it off and give it to a complete stranger. Ali is still a very generous and giving person.

Winning Is a Learned Behavior

One great motivator is the avoidance of pain. Try to avoid anything that is painful. As a boxer I was motivated more by not wanting to lose than the accolades of success. What made me perform at my best was I just didn't like to lose. I just didn't want to lose. That was more important to me than winning. I did not want to experience the pain of losing especially when you are on television and the world is watching. How many times have you seen George Foreman still knocking me out on television? Like many sports, the loss may have been several years ago but people keep reminding you or showing that video clip. It still hurts like it was yesterday.

So to avoid pain or to be happy we win to achieve different levels of success. After you enjoy winning you really don't want to lose. Winning becomes a habit. You expect to win. You expect to get that contract for your firm and when you do it just adds to the success you already have. You will find that winning is a learned behavior. Start learning today on how to become successful tomorrow.

"Why is it so hard for so many to realize that winners are usually the ones who work harder, work longer and, as a result, perform better?

—John Wooden- College Football Coach

Start At the Bottom

Look at the parallel to boxing and business. My first professional fight I was eighteen (18) years old. That is about the same age most people leave high school and seek employment. My job was boxing. You may choose to be a mechanic or a construction worker. It is a choice we make that many times dictates our future.

I started at the bottom of the list of professional fighters and worked my way up rather quickly to get to the top rated fighters. Whether you know it or not your bosses, competitors will rate you but most likely not with a number. It's all about your performance, ability, and experience.

If you work for Ford Motor Company and you are eighteen (18) years old with none or very little experience, they are not going to make you the CEO and pay you millions of dollars to run the company on your first day. I started at the bottom in boxing, just like the assembly line worker at Ford.

After a few years on the job they see you may have talent and the company slowly moves you up. In boxing that is the case most of the time. Your first fight is probably at some county fair and you are one of the six (6) fights scheduled that night. You have very little skills but you are eager learn and taste your first victory.

My teaching point here is to be successful you have to pay your dues. Those dues require you to work hard and receive very little notoriety or compensation. That is why it is important to always be the best at what you do. You have the chance to shine in boxing or business. Do you want to be a shining star or a star that never shined? It's your choice from your first day on the job. How hard do you really want to work? You can choose to be a star performer or just some guy or girl that comes to work and does just the minimum.

Winning Environment

It is the exact same principle in boxing as in life. If you surround yourself with other people that are progressive, creative, energetic, highly motivated and honest, how do you think you will run your life?

There is a quote in the boxing business. If you hang around with dogs that have fleas, you will get fleas.

I wanted to train in the toughest boxing club available. Why, because I wanted to surround myself, like the business executive, with the best boxers in the area. I wanted to learn from the best. They are all proven champions who are all on their way up. That's who I wanted to surround myself with. Those boxers are hungry and are all working hard to get to the top. Surround yourself with the best minds and people who want to get somewhere in life.

One positive point to make about them is that they looked out for each other. I wouldn't hurt any of them nor would they hurt me sparring. We are all in this together and hopefully we will all reach the top one day. You want to surround yourself with winners, not losers.

Five Characteristics of a Winner:

- **Patience**
  This is working now for a future tomorrow. The price of success is paid up front.

- **Self confidence**
  Winners believe in themselves and have a great deal of self confidence.

- **Risk-takers**

  Winners are not afraid of the unknown. They go where no man has gone before. They are not afraid to fail.

- **Work extremely hard**

  Working hard is a lot easier when you love what you are doing and it helps other people.

- **Determination**

  Winners focus on winning and not losing. They give everything they have for the win.

Mistakes

Everyone makes mistakes. The winning principle is to learn from your mistakes. Don't make the same mistake again. In the fight game, one mistake could end your career. One mistake within your company can create havoc and could cause your company to go into bankruptcy. The secret is don't get hit with the big shots, take the small ones and learn from them. Looking back I should have fought George Foreman when he was 55 and not 45. I might have won that fight. That's a little humor folks.

Put It in Writing

One lesson in life that everyone should abide by is, if it deals with money, put it in writing. Prior to any fight there is always a contract. The contracts are for me and my manager, trainer and corner man.

There is another contract for the other fighter, merchandise, and other contracts for pay per view, the location the event is held, sponsors etc. The written document outlines who gets what after the fight. It also outlines specifics before the fight. Everything is in writing.

Boxing is business and business is business. Sometimes it's just hundreds of dollars and other times it could be hundreds of millions of dollars. Learn to put everything in writing at an early age in your career. That way there is no interpretation of what I thought you said.

You will learn as I did, if it involves money, I have one rule, put it in writing. Put the contract or understanding in writing in a language that everyone understands. I don't care if it is your father or sister, put it in writing. Put it in writing and make sure that everyone understands the agreement. Once everyone has had a chance to read it and everyone understands what is said then have everyone sign it.

Remember sometimes people just forget. It happens with age or if you are too busy. What you talked about last week or last year is easily forgotten, especially the little things. All you have to say at the beginning of your meetings or negotiations is, "Even though we are all friends and family, let's be smart about this, so there is no misunderstanding later. Let's put it in writing and have everyone involved sign the agreement. That way we will never have a disagreement over what was said."

When I fought George Foreman my trainer was Teddy Atlas. At the end of the fight I discovered that I was only going to receive one-third of the total purse. I didn't realize the boxing promoter was taking one third and Teddy Atlas got his one third and the guy who actually did the boxing (that would be me) received only one third of the total purse.

I was guaranteed 10 million dollars. So I was to receive a little over 3 million dollars but after taxes and expenses I only received 1.6 million dollars. That may sound like a lot of money but a boxer only has the big pay days later in his career and you only fight two or three times a year. I could have handled the negotiations for that fight a little better.

The important thing is to protect yourself and put it in writing. It is just good business. Not everyone you deal with is trustworthy, especially when you are dealing with millions of dollars.

Prepare for Next Year Starting Today

Very few boxing fans remember my first pro fight. I told you his name earlier in this book. After knocking out Adrian Riggs I went undefeated that year. During that year I was extremely busy and won the World Boxing Organizations (WBO) Light Heavyweight title my first year as a pro. The next year I fought six (6) times and each time I defended the title and knocked out all of my opponents.

I was one of only a few boxers in history to win their first professional 20 fights by a knock out. In the history of boxing there are only a handful of professional boxers to accomplish that record. How was I able to knock out my first twenty (20) opponents? It wasn't because I was lucky. It wasn't because the competition was soft. It was because I prepared myself for each fight relentlessly.

If you want to be a CEO of a blue chip company that job title and huge responsibility is not just handed to you. You have to earn it through hard work and preparation. It is a process much like the new boxer and that is learning new skills today that you may use five years from now. If you prepare yourself for success, it will come.

Don't' Make Mistakes

This is easier said than done. In business or boxing one crucial mistake can cripple your company's chances for success. After all these years of hard work and investment you do one thing wrong and it costs you everything. Try not to make those mistakes. Make the little ones that can be fixed.

Another example of a mistake that is very relative to me as a boxer is when you are winning and success is at your finger tips. You relax or you get over confident and you make a life changing mistake.

This happened to me during the George Foreman fight. I was ahead on all three score cards. I had won every round. We were in the 10th round. I had less than 8 minutes left before the bell would sound for the end of the fight. George was tired and he needed a knock out to win the fight. I dropped my guard for one moment and he hit me with a power right hand. It dazed me. He did it a second time a little harder and down I went.

That was the first time in my life I had lost a fight. If I had won that night in Las Vegas you and your family would be eating off the Double "M" Michael Moorer Lean Cooking Grills and not George's product. Do you know he made more money selling the grills than he did as a boxer? One mistake cost me hundreds of millions of dollars. My advice to you, make the little ones and not the big ones.

It is important for you to capitalize on these moments in time that come by every five years. Sometimes they surprise you and sometimes you expect it. Maybe you have a chance to get a promotion or that part in a movie. The key is to prepare for the opportunity when it presents itself and be ready. Are you ready? I thought I was.

Staying On Top

Now that you are successful, you will find that half of the people around you are excited about your good fortune and the other half of the people around you can't wait for you to fail. They are saying to themselves, "What do you have that I don't have." Staying on top is actually harder than getting there.

If you are an actor, you are only as good as your last movie. If you have a pizza business and hire a new cook and he doesn't make great pies, you lose your customers. It only takes one bad meal in a restaurant to ruin your reputation. You can never coast on your laurels.

I had just beat Evander Holyfield for the heavyweight title and not more than a day or two later I am getting offers, threats, challenges, to defend the heavyweight title. Hell, I had just won the title yesterday. I really wanted to enjoy it for a few days before I committed myself to another fight.

It's funny. Once you make it to the top of anything (tennis, CEO, Police Chief, soccer etc.) some people just can't wait to see you fall. There is always somebody standing in line to take what you have. They are lining up to get the chance to knock out the new champ. I guess it's just Mother Nature.

It will be difficult to satisfy everyone once you have reached the top of your profession. Sometimes it may be difficult to satisfy yourself. People expect more from you now that "you have made it." The pressure is on you to perform. I can do better. I can make more money. I can take that guy. I can make a better computer or I can go faster. Here is a piece of advice. Satisfy yourself and nobody else. Don't live your life for other people. Do what makes you happy. When it is all said and done, it will just be you in the end. Take care of yourself.

"The secret of success is to make your vocation your vacation."

—Mark twain

Prepare For Success

If you work hard enough and long enough you can be successful. Winning is a direct relationship to your talent and how much effort you put forth to be successful. You can have talent but if you lack the confidence and drive for success, that talent will die with you.

There is no guarantee that whatever your endeavor is, you will be successful. Sometimes it's hard work, a great idea, your talent or the product itself that determines your success. But whatever you do expect to succeed. Have that vision of seeing yourself on top. See yourself a winner and think about it daily. Write it down and think about your success. Psychologists have proven that you become what you think about.

Success is not guaranteed if you just work hard. That is the physical part of your climb to the top. After having done the physical part there is a second half that is just as important. That is the mental or psychological part. In boxing you study your opponent ... knowing his strengths and look for his weaknesses. In business you study your competition. How did they get to the top? What are they doing now? Remember, luck is simply where preparation and opportunity meet. You have to be ready to take advantage of that opportunity when it comes knocking.

Preparation is paramount to being successful as a boxer or a business professional. You don't step into the ring unless you have prepared yourself physically and mentally. You run the miles, do the sit ups, eat right, put in the thousands of rounds of sparring and only then do you feel confident and ready.

How many business people do you know that start a business or an acting career and plan on failing. They say to themselves, "I know this restaurant is not going to make it, but that's OK." That would be ridiculous. Plan on winning and being successful. When you begin your journey to achieve your goals, it is so important to focus on one day at a time. Make that one day productive and get something accomplished.

I want you to plan for success. See yourself at the top so when you get there it is not a surprise. Look at how many people who win the lottery blow through the millions of dollars and are broke within a few years ... and they are worse off now than before they won. Success came to them but they were not ready for it.

One of our investigative clients hit the Florida lottery. He split $36 million dollars with another ticket holder. Since winning the lottery his wife has tried to poison him, his relatives will not talk to him and he became an alcoholic. He told me that winning the lottery was the worst day of his life. He tried to give it back but his attorney talked him out of it. Money does not always bring happiness.

How to Make Money

After I retired from boxing, I opened an investigative agency called Double "M" Investigations & Protection Services. My nickname as a boxer was "Double M" or my initials from Michael Moorer. The investigative company conducts background checks, locates, asset searches, security guards, personal protection and surveillances.

I started the investigative agency because I love the cloak and dagger investigative world. We also provide bodyguards to corporate executives and high profile people. It is a lot of fun and very profitable.

How do we make money? The answer is by duplicating yourself five (5) or six (6) times. You don't do the work but hire other people, under your supervision, to make you money. Smart business executives leverage their time. You can only be at one place at one time. Hire people to work for you, train them to be professional and put them in the field for you.

A good example would be my business of investigations and surveillance. If I am on surveillance for eight (8) hours and charge $100 an hour, I make $800 for the day. It's not the 10 million I made for one fight but in today's economy it is not that bad of an income for one day.

But, what if I hired six investigators? Each investigator works eight (8) hours on surveillance. At the end of the day my gross is six (6) investigators at eight (8) hours and $100 per hour. Now I am grossing $4,800 for the day. After paying each of the investigators $50 dollars an hour at the end of the day my profit is $2,400 for the day and I stayed in the office all day. If I have a good week and continued surveillance for five of the seven days of the week my gross for the week is $12,000.

Boy do things change. I use to make $12,000 just to show up at a function for an hour, sign a few autographs, and take a few pictures. The only difference is this is what I love doing now after boxing. I like the business and enjoy providing my services to people who need help. This is as close to being a police officer as I can get.

This scenario can be duplicated if you are a house painter, produce silk screened or digital T-shirts, or have a law office firm with 20 attorneys.

The Price of Success

When you get older and reflect on your life one day you might ask yourself, "Was it all worth it?" The real question is, "are you satisfied on how you got the success"?

The Dalai Lama said, "Judge your success by what you had to give up in order to get it."

As a boxer I did give up a lot. I can look back and truthfully say my boxing career was costly to my personal relationships and my family. I had a personal quest that burned deep inside me. At times during my career I have to say my personal and family life suffered. I can't change my past. All I can do is try to be the best father I can be when we are together now.

To be a winner and successful sometimes have to choose a path that is different from your friends. You are determined to actualize your dreams and often other people get hurt. No fault but my own, but I made choices that I must live by today. If you want to be successful, it is going to be difficult, and painful, as it was for me. You will satisfy your dream but at the sacrifice of your personal life. That is just the facts of life.

When you do reach your goal of financial success not all of your peers, associates and friends will welcome your new fortune. Many will ask, "Why him/her and not me. They are not smarter than I am?" It is a hard fact of life that some people want you to fail. That is why it is important to forge ahead and don't resent your friends who have found love, financial rewards or have a great family. Be happy for them, because, not all of the wealth in the world can buy you happiness. You will make hard choices that will change your life forever.

Share Your Success

This is not a very well known story but it is true. Donald Trump was traveling on the highway one day and his car actually broke down. An unknown man came to his aid and really didn't know who he was. I believe the story goes that he got the Donald going and gave Mr. Trump a business card. As he left he said, "If you need anything else just give me a call."

Without telling anyone Donald Trump found out where the Good Samaritan lived, called the bank and paid off the man's mortgage on his house. Trump did all this without telling anyone. If fact he didn't even tell the owner of the house. When he sent in his next mortgage payment the bank sent it back. Only then was he told that the mortgage on his house had been paid.

The Good Samaritan told someone and after a while the story was in the news. The point is that Donald Trump didn't do it for publicity or personal gain. An unknown person aided him because he wanted to help. For that Mr. Trump paid off his $60,000 house mortgage. Why, because he could. Don't show your success. Share your success.

Success in Life

If you are looking for the answer to success in your life time you don't have very far to go. The next time you are on a commercial flight, a bus, the mall or in the park look for an elderly couple or individual sitting down on the bench or seat. Take the seat next to them. I would recommend that they are in their 70' or 80's. Once you introduced yourself and found out a little about them, ask them the true meaning of life or success. You will be surprised at their answer.

The elderly person will not tell you how rich they are or the vast fortunes they made during their life time. They will not tell you about the house in France, or the one in Colorado and the other home in Florida. They will also not tell you about their rise to fame or riches. That is not what is really important or what life is made of.

But they will tell you about their family and grand children. How they should have spent more holidays at home with the wife and their children rather than working. They will tell you they were working and missed several birthday's. They will also tell you about the Christmas's they missed.

They will tell you it was a long time ago but it still bothers them that they weren't there. They also might mention the vacations they didn't take because they were working so hard. That is what life really is about and not the vast fortunes you amassed. In your life you have to have balance. Find the time to make the money and at the same time enjoy your success with the one's you love.

As an example take a look at Garth Brooks. Garth is one of the most famous performers in country music and music itself. For years he traveled and sacrificed for himself and his family. Then one day he just stays at home. Quits the music industry and now is enjoying taking his children to school and doing the things that dad's do. He must to have spoken to a lot of elderly folks, because he did it right.

What you will find is that true success is not something you can buy but something you share with other people.

"He who is __not__ courageous enough to take risks will accomplish nothing in life."

—Muhammad Ali

Writing this book and trying to choose quotes that are appropriate has been a lot of fun. I have used the quotes of some really famous people. I really love the message they are trying to convey. But, what really amazes me is how gifted a boxer Muhammad Ali was in the ring and out of the ring. His quotes are remarkably profound and at the same time inspirational. I think he is a truly great man.

Success and Giving Back

No act of kindness, no matter how small is ever wasted. If you look at the big financial winners in life they all use their money to help people. Look what Microsoft giant Bill Gates and his lovely wife Melinda are doing? They are saving lives and are helping people who have aids or HIV. That is the end product of being successful. It's the stuff money can buy.

Mike Tyson gave an interview to a sports magazine years after he finished boxing. The reporter asked him if he had a plan for his future now that he was finished with boxing. Mike Tyson replied, "If there is a big plan now, it's just to give and care for the people who deserve it. I just want to be of service to people, I need to help. I need to have something, finally, that I can offer people in this world"

> *I think that Muhammad Ali said it best. "Service to others is the rent you pay for your room here on earth."*

Key Points of Round 12:   Fighting for Success

- Be thankful for what you have.
- Don't just show your success, share your success.
- No act of kindness is unrecognized.
- Make the little mistakes not the big ones.
- Getting to the top is easy. Staying there is difficult.

Progressive Action Steps (PAS)   Completed

1. Prepare for your success   ☐

2. Share your success   ☐

3. Find balance in your life   ☐

4. Today I shared my success with someone else   ☐

In conclusion-the decision

I want to thank you for taking the time to read this book. I am just one example of what a person can do that is motivated and commits himself/herself to one goal. Notice I said one goal. You must be specific and directed when you decide exactly what you want to do with your life. During the majority of my career, I was still standing after the 12th round.

The decision to make your dream a reality is all up to you. I hope by now many of you have reviewed each chapter and have taken the time to write down your action goals and responses. Each one of you has the personal power within yourself to raise the bar, live better and do more with your life than you ever expected. You can take your financial success to a level you never dreamed of. I don't care what people say, the dollar still rules the world. Go make it happen. Start today and thanks for your time.

May the road rise up to meet you,
May the wind always be at your back,
May the sun shine warm upon your face,
May the rain fall soft upon your fields,
And until we meet again may God hold you in the palm of his hand.

I appreciate you taking the time in purchasing and reading our book 12 Rounds to Success. Best of luck to you as you change your life for the better.

Thank you,

Michael Moorer
"Double M"

Seminars and Speaking Engagements

Michael Moorer and Walter Philbrick are available for corporate seminars, book fairs and or personal events. Mr. Moorer is available to attend your function. He can sign books and autographs, have a photograph session with your clients, and talk about the book and his career in boxing.

Please give Mr. Moorer advanced notice if you want him to attend as a guest speaker. The co-author Walter Philbrick is also available for book signings and training seminars.

To contact Michael Moorer or Walter Philbrick for speaking engagements, motivational seminars or book signings call:

Phone: (954) 922-9258
Toll Free: 1-800-510-0820
Email: FL911Store@aol.com
Ask for: Walter Philbrick for Michael Moorer

Acknowledgment and Appreciation

I would like to thank George Foreman for writing the introduction of this book. His time and contribution is greatly appreciated.

I also want to thank Ms. Mynde Manfredi for taking the time formatting and assisting with the editing of this publication.

Printed in Great Britain
by Amazon.co.uk, Ltd.,
Marston Gate.